BIRMINGHAM-BRISTOL
PORTRAIT OF A FAMOUS MIDLAND ROUTE

Part One
Birmingham to Cheltenham

STEPHEN MOURTON & BOB PIXTON

This pictorial work on the Birmingham-Bristol route is being published in two parts:
Part One herewith covers Birmingham to Cheltenham, including the line through Worcester.
Part Two will look at Cheltenham to Bristol and Bath via Gloucester.
The whole is expected to comprise around three hundred photographs, mainly from the steam era, which will form a comprehensive record of this fascinating, vitally important and very busy part of the British railway system.

RUNPAST PUBLISHING

Front cover: **Birmingham New Street, 1949.** Two 4-4-0s get ready to attack the gradient out to Church Road Junction. The leading loco stills displays LMS on the tender, while the other has the full BR title, with cabside number M935. The 'M' appendage was a short-lived early BR scheme, soon replaced by one which added 40000 to the LMS number, so 935 became 40935. The loco was from Bristol Barrow Road depot, code 22A, creating an ideal image for this book about the Midland's route from Birmingham to Bristol. No.5 signal box is in the background in this picture; it was the largest box at New Street, with 153 levers, and was staffed by three men in daytime and two at night. *H C Casserley*

Back cover – top: **Worcester, 1928.** An old single-framed Kirtley, rebuilt Johnson, 2-4-0, still wearing its Midland Railway number 97, sits at Shrub Hill station with an exquisitely ornate GWR lamp and post in the foreground. Both locomotive and lamp show the Victorian love of design for what are essentially utilitarian items. The LMS shed at Worcester was closed in 1932, after which the GWR shed played host to visiting Midland engines. *R S Carpenter collection*

Back cover – middle: **Bromsgrove South, early 1950s.** A grubby, leaking Leeds Holbeck 'Jubilee' 45589 *Gwalior* is in charge of the down 'Devonian', one of the two named expresses to be seen here, the other being 'The Pines Express'. For some years the down 'Devonian' stopped at Worcester, but the up train took the direct route. This train's greatest days were from 1937, after introduction of faster schedules, until the outbreak of war, when it did Leeds to Bristol in 4 hours 40 minutes. Standards of cleanliness and maintenance for Holbeck and Bristol Barrow Road 'Jubilees', which were used on the up 'Devonian', improved markedly later in the 1950s. Behind the train, a number of Lickey bankers are ready for duty. Another LMS improvement was quadrupling the line from here to Stoke Works, which came into use in May 1933. *Real Photographs*

Back cover – bottom: **Camp Hill goods depot.** Camp Hill holds a significant place in the history of the Birmingham & Gloucester Railway, as trains from Gloucester started running into here, the Birmingham terminus, on 17 December 1840, having overcome the obstacle posed by the Lickey Hills. It was a short distance from Camp Hill to join up with the London & Birmingham Railway and a triumphant entry to Curzon Street station in August the following year. The site, by then on a short dead end branch off the main line, became the B & G's Birmingham goods depot – though it is said that some goods trains still conveyed third-class passengers to and from Camp Hill! – and remained in business until February 1966, when closed by BR. The LMS goods and grain warehouse seen here dates from the 1890s. *R S Carpenter collection*

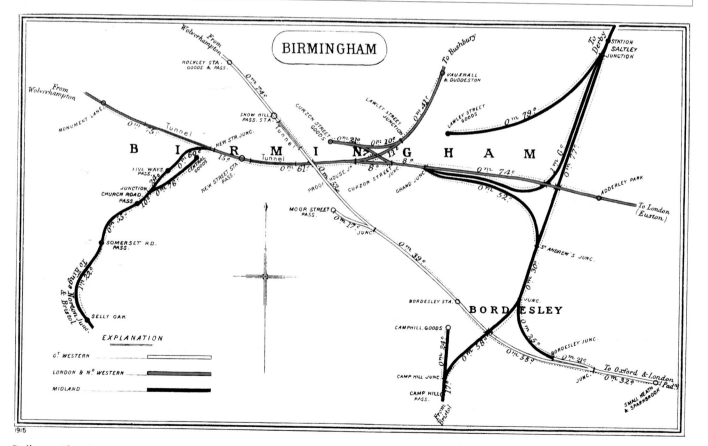

Railway Clearing House map of 1915 showing the Midland Railway routes at New Street and Camp Hill, together with GWR and LNWR lines in the area. The Midland had running powers from Grand Junction to New Street Junction and New Street station was made joint with the LNWR from 1897.

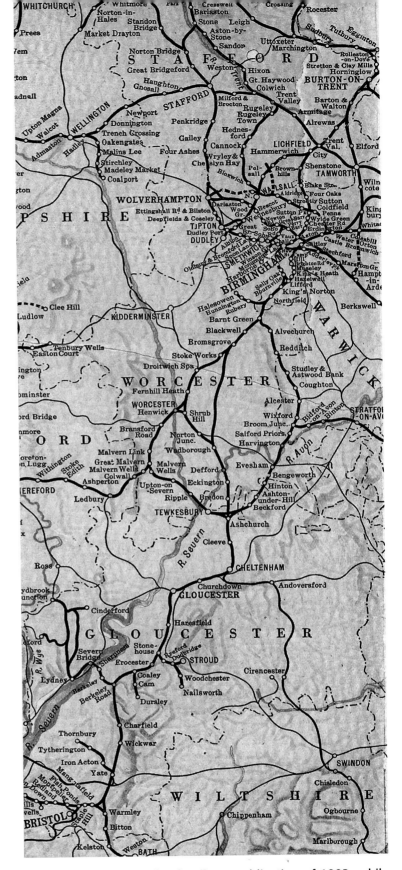

The map on the left is taken from a Midland Railway publication of 1903, while the other, giving a wider view of the route and its connections, is from a 1934 LMS timetable. Mileages from Birmingham New Street: to Cheltenham Lansdown 45 and a quarter miles; to Bristol Temple Meads 88 and three-quarter miles; to Bath 93 and a half miles. Distance from Washwood Heath Sidings to Westerleigh Sidings 83 miles. Trains via Worcester Shrub Hill – extra 2 and a half miles.

Birmingham New Street, mid 1950s. A bird's-eye view of the station evokes some pleasant nostalgia! Birmingham Corporation buses, cars in great variety and the steam age station – below street level, gloomy, but for many still preferable to the concrete creation that replaced it in the 1960s. The central Queen's Drive into the station which separated the North West side, on the left, from the Midland side, on the right, is prominent. The Midland part, dating from the 1880s, has the original domed roof, while the London & North Western side's similar roof has been replaced. After the 1885 extension, New Street was claimed to be the biggest station in the British Isles. At the time of its centenary celebrations in 1954, New Street was said to be the fourth busiest station on the London Midland Region. There were 190 trains in, and 180 out, on weekdays, while 3 million people a year used the booking offices and the station master had a staff of 600.

R S Carpenter collection

Introduction

The railway from Birmingham to Bristol has long been a vital artery in the national network. The route's importance has not diminished over the years and it continues to support a heavy flow of passenger and goods traffic even in these days of near universal car ownership and the unceasing drone of articulated trucks along the M5 motorway, its equivalent in road terms.

This book looks at the line in some detail, particularly during steam days which lasted for over 125 years from 1840. We have tried to resist the all too easy temptation to stray away from the main Midland line – so just a quick look at New Street before setting off; a brief view of the branch which goes off at Barnt Green through Redditch, Alcester and Evesham before rejoining the main line at Ashchurch; not allowing the famous Lickey incline to take up a disproportionate part of the book; barely a glimpse of the GWR's operations at Worcester; or dwelling on the alternative route between Birmingham and Bristol provided by the GWR. Most of these subjects have already had a book, or number of books, devoted to them, but our main theme has mainly been covered in magazine articles or books which deal with bits of the line. So we felt it was about time to compile this tome dealing with the Midland route from Birmingham to Cheltenham, including the 'Worcester Loop' – very much an integral part of the system – with another to follow on the line from Cheltenham to Bristol.

This part includes the Camp Hill route, which was the original line up to Birmingham from Cheltenham, Gloucester and Bristol, becoming the main freight artery between those places, so is every bit as important as the passenger line from New Street.

Inevitably some pictures have been published before, but we have tried to provide interesting details in the captions, often referring to operational matters as well as the usual historical details of opening and closing dates.

Stephen Mourton, Bob Pixton, July 2001

Contents

© 2001 Stephen Mourton and Bob Pixton

Published by Runpast Publishing, 10 Kingscote Grove, Cheltenham, Gloucestershire GL51 6JX

Typesetting and reproduction by Viners Wood Associates – 01452 812813
Printed in England by The Amadeus Press Ltd., Cleckheaton

ISBN 1 870754 53 0

The Making of the Route

Proposals for a railway from Birmingham to Gloucester and Bristol were mooted from the mid-1820s onwards, but nothing much happened until 1833 when the renowned I.K.Brunel undertook a survey. It was 1835 before things really got underway, with the issue of a prospectus for the Birmingham and Gloucester Railway Company (B&G), which attracted a lot of money, with the share issue being oversubscribed. The Bill for this railway was approved and incorporated by an Act of Parliament in April 1836. It bypassed the town of Worcester and proposed a branch off the main line to Tewkesbury, while its outstanding feature was to be the ascent of the Lickey Hills by locomotive power, not considered practicable by either Brunel or George Stephenson.

Captain William Scarth Moorsom surveyed the route, becoming the company's resident engineer and a pivotal figure in the subsequent success of the railway. Bromsgrove, at the foot of the Lickey Hills, was the railway's base, the workshops were built here, as was the principal locomotive running shed. Most of the early locomotives for the line were imported from Norris of Philadelpia, USA, whose engines were considered by the B&G as being the most suitable for climbing the Lickey incline. The first one arrived in March 1839 and, because the B&G was not ready, it was tested on the Grand Junction Railway; however the loco's performance did not come up to expectations.

After various trial runs, the B&G opened between Cheltenham and Bromsgrove on 24 June 1840. There were intermediate stations at Ashchurch, with a branch from there to Tewkesbury (opened 21 July 1840); Bredon; Eckington; Defford; Spetchley; Droitwich (later Droitwich Road); and Stoke (later Stoke Works). This route, which came to be known in later years as the 'Old Road', bypassed Worcester. And there was still no railway over the Lickey Hills, passengers and goods having to go by road transport from Bromsgrove to Birmingham. The line up the Lickey eventually opened on 17 September 1840 and went on to Cofton Farm, a temporary terminus eight miles from Birmingham. Further progress towards Birmingham had to await the completion of the 440-yards long, and narrow, Cofton tunnel. On the incline, trains initially tended to have an assisting engine in front of the train engine, rather than being banked at the rear. The first engines for this assisting work were five of the famous 4-2-0s by William Norris of Philadelphia, USA – three delivered in 1840 and two in 1842, all being converted to saddle tanks. There were other 4-2-0 Norris

locos, built in England as well as the USA, which worked on the line, along with four 6-wheeled engines by Forrester of Liverpool. The railway extended from Cheltenham to Gloucester on 4 November 1840, giving a boost to traffic potential, as a large amount of Birmingham's supplies came through the docks at Gloucester. Discussions had already taken place with the proposed Bristol and Gloucester Railway about forming a single entity to run throughout from Birmingham to Bristol, thus forming the only direct rail communication between the north and west of England, and making the route one of the most important in the country.

The locomotive construction shops of the B&G were opened at Bromsgrove in 1840.

A tragedy occurred on Tuesday 10 November 1840 when an 0-2-2T locomotive named *Surprise* blew up at Bromsgrove, resulting in the deaths of the locomotive works foreman, Joseph Rutherford, aged 32, and an engine driver, Thomas Scaife, aged 28. *Surprise* had been on trial, having been offered to the B&G at a knock-down price. To this day, there are memorials to the two men at a churchyard in Bromsgrove. The one for Scaife records that he was 'highly esteemed by his fellow workmen for his amiable qualities, and his death will be long lamented by all those who had the pleasure of his acquaintance.'

On 17 December 1840, the railway extended from Cofton Farm to a terminus at Camp Hill, Birmingham.

Moorsom became Chairman of the B&G in February 1841. After a period of poor supervision and maintenance of the company's engines, resulting in just a handful being able to work the line without breaking down, J E McConnell was appointed engine super-intendent and reliability was considerably improved. A nice touch was that locos were often named after places on or near the line, such as *Ashchurch, Cheltenham, Defford, Spetchley, Droitwich, Pershore* etc. From 17 August 1841 the B&G ran to the London and Birmingham Railway's station at Birmingham Curzon Street, by which time it was running eight trains each way on weekdays. From 1 May 1842, trains from Gloucester changed engines at Bromsgrove, a banking engine tackled the incline on its own, coming off at Blackwell, where another engine took over for the run into Birmingham. From November 1842, the B&G and L&B combined in running coaches through from Euston to Gloucester via Curzon Street. (This connection remained for over a hundred years, in that until 1952 it was possible to book tickets from Gloucester Eastgate to

Birmingham Curzon Street. What an imposing edifice! Grand Junction Railway trains from Liverpool and Manchester began to use this station in 1838. The London & Birmingham Railway ran through trains between Euston and here from September 1838, while the Birmingham & Gloucester made it to Curzon Street from August 1841. The B&G became part of the Midland Railway, but the other two were amalgamated into the London & North Western Railway in 1846 and it was the latter company which decided to build a new station first called Navigation Street, changed later to New Street, which opened in 1854. Curzon Street survived as a goods station and the edifice is still with us, a preserved monument to those early railway days in Birmingham.　　　　　*R&CHS*

Euston via Birmingham New Street for the same fare as Gloucester Central to Paddington via Swindon.)

The B&G's ambition to connect with Bristol was partly realised in July 1844 when the Bristol & Gloucester Railway opened its line between those two places. Unfortunately through running was not possible because the B&G was standard gauge while the Bristol & Gloucester was built to Brunel's broad gauge. Chaos and confusion reigned at Gloucester as passengers and goods transferred between trains. From January 1845 the two railways operated as one – the Birmingham and Bristol Railway – with a common board of directors, though no company with that name was ever formed.

In June 1845, a brand new banking locomotive designed by McConnell emerged from Bromsgrove Works. Named *Great Britain*, it was an 0-6-0 saddle tank, said to be the most powerful locomotive in the country at the time, weighing around 30 tons, and proved to be a great success at its allotted task. Other new locomotives for both standard gauge, such as two 2-4-0s in 1846, and broad gauge, came from outside

manufacturers including Vulcan Foundry.

The newly-formed Midland Railway took over the working of the Birmingham and Bristol Railway in May 1845, before absorbing it on 3 August 1846. This amalgamation thwarted the GWR's designs on extending the broad gauge northwards. But the MR had to contend with the change of gauge at Gloucester and inherited the broad gauge locomotives and rolling stock which operated from Bristol. This state of affairs continued until 29 May 1854 from which date the Midland operated only on standard gauge.

It was 1846 when some railway engineers met at Bromsgrove to witness locomotive trials on the Lickey incline. Sheltering from a rain shower in a platelayer's hut, their discussions led directly to the formation of the Institution of Mechanical Engineers at the Queen's Hotel, Birmingham in January 1847, whose first president was George Stephenson.

From 5 October 1850 the Midland used the 'Worcester Loop', as it had running powers over the Oxford, Worcester and Wolverhampton Railway's line from

Abbot's Wood Junction, on the B&G, to Worcester, which opened on that date. Until then, the city of Worcester had been connected by road coach to the MR's station at Spetchley on the B&G route. From Worcester Shrub Hill, which later became a joint MR/GWR station, Midland trains used the OWW main line to Droitwich, before taking the branch to Stoke Prior (later Stoke Works) Junction – opened on 18 February 1852 – where the loop rejoined the B&G; the total distance from Abbot's Wood was 13 miles 70 chains (the distance by the 'Old Road' bypassing Worcester was 11 miles 26 chains). The station at Stoke Works was never served by its owning company, the OWW, only by the Midland, a situation which continued even after the OWW had been absorbed by the GWR. Until 1 June 1880, all Midland expresses went through Worcester, but from that date onwards, some reverted to the 'Old Road', leaving fewer services to call at Shrub Hill, setting the pattern for subsequent years.

The impressive new Birmingham New Street station opened on 1 June 1854, owned by the London and North Western Railway, but available also to the Midland Railway from 1 July that year, under powers granted to the Birmingham & Gloucester in earlier days. However most Midland trains between Derby and Gloucester bypassed New Street, detaching or attaching coaches for it at Camp Hill or Saltley, just some local services used it. Curzon Street became a goods station, apart from being used for excursion trains. Due to increasing traffic as Birmingham expanded, an extension was eventually built at New Street for the Midland Railway, first coming into operation in February 1885, though it was October 1889 before all Midland trains commenced using the 'new' side. New Street was made a joint station between the MR and LNWR in April 1897, with joint management.

Important improvements the previous year for Midland trains were the opening of New Street tunnel with lines independent of the LNWR taking the MR to Proof House Junction, also a new curve, Derby Junction to Landor Street Junction, which passed under the LNWR main line; these helped to cut down on delays in the approaches to New Street from Derby.

The secondary route which left the main line at Barnt Green for Redditch was opened on 19 September 1859 by the Redditch Railway, being the first part of the loop

Blackwell. This is the view from the up platform and shows the severity of the Lickey incline, the line literally disappears down the gradient of 1 in 37 and three-quarters. There is a sign in front of the hut on the down side which states *Goods trains to stop to pin down brakes*. In the BR Sectional Appendix book, the special instructions for descending the Lickey took up just over two pages, while those for ascending it occupied less than a page. So while most articles over the years have focussed on the going up, the going down was more problematical from an operating viewpoint, if not from a lineside observer's view. Heavy trains descending the incline sometimes had banking locos ahead of the train engine to provide increased braking power. One such in 1962 was a working of steel ingots from Tees-side to South Wales, around 1300 tons of train.   *R S Carpenter collection*

Bromsgrove station. The view looking up the 'straight as a die' 2 miles 4 chains of 1 in 37.75 incline was daunting for engine crews, especially if their loco was not doing too well for steam. But at least they could – and often did – place great reliance on the bankers to help them and maybe even recover steam if they took it easy. The building on the right behind the station is part of the former Birmingham & Gloucester Railway workshop. This was used for wagon building and maintenance in Midland days and later and, apart from Derby Works, was said to be better equipped for the work than other similar MR facilities. *J A Peden collection*

line which eventually went on from Redditch to Alcester (opened 4 May 1868); Alcester to Evesham (opened 16 June 1866); and Evesham to Ashchurch (opened 1 July 1864) where it rejoined the main Birmingham to Bristol line. The sections from Redditch to Evesham and Evesham to Ashchurch were built by the famous contractor Thomas Brassey. By the time the 'Gloucester Loop' as it was known, became a through route, it was all operated by the Midland. Though there was a stopping passenger service from New Street to Ashchurch via Redditch and Evesham, the loop was not normally used for regular long-distance expresses. It was useful in enabling freight trains to avoid the Lickey if required. The section from Ashchurch through Evesham to Broom Junction saw quite a lot of iron ore and steel train workings in BR days and LMS banana trains from Avonmouth took this route to get onto the Stratford & Midland Junction line and eventually head for London. From 1891, the Midland Railway ran freights from London St Pancras to Bristol utilising the route, a service which continued into LMS days.

Another line on the railway map which helped to complete the modern Birmingham and Bristol route was the Birmingham West Suburban Railway, running from Lifford, going under the Camp Hill line, then via Bournville, Selly Oak and Church Road to a station at Birmingham Granville Street, authorised in May 1871, but not opened throughout until 3 April 1876. The line threaded its way alongside an older form of transport, the Worcester & Birmingham canal. An extension from Church Road Junction to Birmingham New Street was authorised by an act of 1881 and opened on 1 July 1885 (when Granville Street closed); it was difficult and expensive to build and operate with several dank tunnels and a gradient of 1 in 75/80 out of New Street to Church Road Junction, very taxing for locomotives on heavy trains in steam days, with a banking engine sometimes giving assistance on departure from the station. The completion of this connection meant that trains coming from the north and going on to Gloucester could run through New Street without the need to reverse and depart via the Camp Hill line; Midland express passenger trains starting using it, and New Street station, from 1 October 1885. But while reversal of through Midland trains at Birmingham had now been done away with, it was still necessary at this time at Gloucester, where the MR station was a terminus. (Further details will be included in part two of this work.)

A new piece of track between Bournville to King's Norton opened on 26 September 1885, bypassing the

Hazelwell station. This picture dates from 16 September 1961 as 9F 92052 takes an up freight north. Twenty years after the last passenger trains called, the platforms are still in place. The Camp Hill route has always been the main freight artery through Birmingham and on to Bristol. *Michael Mensing*

slightly longer line via Lifford.

In 1887, the branch from Church Road to Granville Street was extended to the new Central Goods depot. A further change occurred at Lifford in 1891-92 with the excavation of a cutting creating a triangle of lines there, which proved useful operationally.

Thus the Midland Railway's route to Bristol became – at the Birmingham end at least – the one familiar to travellers up to the present day from the North East and Midlands to the West Country and South Wales. It formed a vital part of the Midland Railway's greatest length of continuous line, running from Bath to Carlisle, which at 320 miles was 12 miles more than London St Pancras to Carlisle.

The Midland Railway was shaken up by competition from the GWR in 1908 when the latter started running expresses between Birmingham and Bristol via the Honeybourne line which made significant inroads into the MR's traffic. The two railways engaged in legal disputes, such as over running powers at Yate, which the GWR won; and payment by the MR for using GWR tracks at Worcester, which led to Midland through trains being denied access for a while, with coaches having to be detached at Ashchurch or Bromsgrove for Worcester. Co-operation between the GWR and the London & South

Western Railway over a service from Bournemouth to Birkenhead and Manchester led the MR and London & North Western Railway to introduce a through Manchester-Bournemouth service in 1910 via Birmingham, Bath and the Somerset & Dorset Railway – which in 1927 became the 'Pines Express'. The MR also smartened up timings of its top trains between Derby and Bristol.

The First World War led to some economies on the Midland, such as withdrawal of the passenger service from New Street to Great Malvern and the through coaches from Birmingham to Brecon and Swansea via Worcester and Hereford.

In late 1922, just before the railway grouping leading to the formation of the 'Big Four' companies, the Midland sought parliamentary powers for schemes to improve the line. The plans included improvements at King's Norton and putting in extra running lines between Halesowen Junction and Barnt Green to increase capacity and accelerate train times. A further overdue improvement started in 1926 – the demolition of Cofton Tunnel, said to be the narrowest on the whole of the Midland Railway. It was replaced by a rock cutting, so there were considerable earthworks and a few accidents occurred, resulting in the deaths of navvies. The old tunnel was finally demolished between 26 and 28

January 1929. Even after all this work had been completed, the LMS had more plans for improving the line between Birmingham and Bristol. Trackwork was to be improved to enable heavier loads hauled by more modern engines to use the line. One part of this scheme was adding extra tracks between Bromsgrove and Stoke Works, which was done in 1932/33.

But with the difficult economic circumstances of the early 1930s, the 'Big Four' railway companies instituted the 'Pooling of Traffic Agreements' to reduce duplication of services; one of the products of this was the diversion to other routes of through freight trains which had travelled via Worcester and Hereford to South Wales, leading to the closure of Worcester LMS loco shed in 1932.

The Second World War produced great strains on the route, now more than ever a vital artery, with military activity adding to the very heavy freight traffic and overloaded passenger trains bursting at the seams. The GWR's express passenger service between Birmingham and Bristol via Honeybourne was withdrawn from 25 September 1939 until 1 October 1945, making the Midland route even busier.

After hostilities ceased, along came Nationalisation with opportunities for eliminating duplication of management, routes and services, as well as possible integration of various functions. One new through service on the route was introduced in winter 1952/53, that from Newcastle-on-Tyne to Cardiff and later Swansea. The Western Region took over management of the line northwards to Barnt Green from the London Midland Region, resulting in some motive power changes. Then modernisation introduced diesel locos on the route from 1961, while diesel multiple units had been introduced in the 1950s on Birmingham suburban services out of New Street. Cutbacks started lopping off the branch feeder services, such as the passenger trains from Ashchurch to Upton-on-Severn and to Barnt Green via the Gloucester Loop. On and from 4 January 1965 all intermediate stations on the main line from Bristol to Worcester lost their passenger service except Gloucester, Cheltenham and Ashchurch; further north, Stoke Works and Blackwell shut on and from 18 April 1966. Freight depots and shunting yards were also closing or being modernised.

Pritchatts Road, September 1962. 'Black 5' 44777 powers an up express around a curve on the Birmingham West Suburban line north of Selly Oak alongside the Worcester & Birmingham canal. The tranquil setting belies the fact that New Street station, at the heart of the city, is less than three miles distant. There used to be a station nearby, at Somerset Road for Harborne, but it closed in July 1930.   *A W V Mace collection*

Halesowen Junction, 26 June 1929. LMS Compound 1061 bowls along with a relatively heavy express of mixed stock, indicating through coaches from and to various places. The first vehicle, a fine twelve-wheeled clerestory, is probably a restaurant car; it is frustrating not being able to read the carriage headboard on it. Interestingly, the loco is paired with one of three tenders specially converted for use by engines working the 'Royal Scot' from London to Glasgow and Edinburgh, which competed with the LNER's 'Flying Scotsman' non-stop service introduced in May 1928.

Author's collection

All these changes – and the Western Region's desire to be fully dieselised – accelerated the demise of steam, which became rarer down the line from Birmingham as 1966 progressed. There was no definitive final date for steam working, as on some other parts of BR, it just quietly faded away.

Some familiar parts of the main line also closed – trains no longer worked out of Bristol up the Midland line through Mangotsfield after 1969 and Gloucester Eastgate closed in December 1975, along with the line to Tuffley Junction. Rumours from time to time of electrification from Birmingham to Bristol never came to fruition, though the line has now been electrified from New Street through Bournville to Barnt Green and along the branch to Redditch, following the opening of new stations along the main line at Five Ways, University and Longbridge in 1978. There is talk of electrification of the suburban service to Bromsgrove and possibly beyond, to Worcester.

There were other gains from time to time – High Speed Trains improved journey times on the long-distance through passengers; and a few stations on the way to Bristol, such as Ashchurch and Yate, reopened in recent years.

One thing which has not changed since those first trains ran in 1840 is that Birmingham to Bristol is still a vitally important route for the national rail network.

The historical details in this part relate mainly to the line from Birmingham to Cheltenham. Part 2 will have more on the history of the route from Cheltenham to Bristol.

Steam locos on the route
This brief survey gives an overview and is not intended as an exhaustive list of every type which worked on the route over the years.

The Midland Railway had large numbers of 0-6-0s and these featured during virtually the whole of the steam era. And not just on freights, but also on many passenger and parcels trains. Sheds which provided locos for the line would not hesitate to turn out an 0-6-0 even for long-distance extras, say an excursion from Gloucester to Blackpool or a summer season Saturday relief from Sheffield to Bristol.

2-2-2s provided power for passenger trains from the mid-nineteenth century, while Johnson 4-2-2 'Spinners' were regular power in the later years of the century, being shedded at Saltley, Derby, Gloucester and Bristol. 2-4-0s were ever present, including piloting Johnson and Deeley 4-4-0s, as the Midland favoured double-heading when train tonnages increased.

Various 4-4-0s worked the line in the 1920s – the 1P type could be seen on pilot duties especially on summer Saturdays; 2Ps worked the lighter expresses and those going to Bath; 3Ps had the heavier ones, but did not go to Bath; Compound 4Ps though did not work on the route until after the grouping, when newly-built LMS examples became familiar; the '990' class 4Ps were never recorded, apart from one trialled on the Somerset & Dorset in 1924 (according to historian H C Casserley).

Horwich Moguls started to appear in the late 1920s and 'Baby Scot' 4-6-0s in the 1930s. Ex-LNWR engines sometimes had regular workings down from Birmingham – in 1926 a 'Renown' 4-4-0 hauled a daily stopping passenger to Gloucester. The new Stanier 'Black 5s' appeared on the line in 1935, with some of the class being allocated in 1937 to local sheds Saltley, Gloucester and Bristol. 'Jubilee' 4-6-0s also worked on the line in increasing numbers from the mid-1930s and were the main express power for many years. Stanier 8F 2-8-0s became everyday sights on heavy freights. Somerset & Dorset 2-8-0s were also seen from time to time, especially working to Gloucester or Derby for repairs.

In the Second World War, some old 0-6-0s from the LNER and 4-4-0s from the Southern Railway were on loan at places such as Bristol, Gloucester and Worcester. USATC American 2-8-0s could be seen on freights, while Ashchurch military depot had USATC 0-6-0T, which might possibly be glimpsed in passing.

During BR days, with the exception of types not allowed on the line, such as ex-LMS Pacifics, a wide variety of loco classes could be seen from lots of different sheds on the London Midland, Western, Eastern, North Eastern, Southern and Scottish Regions – a few notable examples are mentioned further on. There were restrictions on ex-GWR types going into New Street station – although some got there in later steam days – and they did work via Camp Hill to Washwood Heath.

'Baby Scot' now officially 'Patriot' class No.45509 *The Derbyshire Yeomanry* was the only one of its type regularly seen on the route for some years in the 1950s, working the daily Nottingham-Bristol morning passenger train, returning with the 4.45pm Bristol-York express. In the late 1950s three more of the class, Nos.45504/06/19, were allocated to Bristol Barrow Road shed.

In the BR era Barrow Road had an allocation of

Barnt Green, late 1920s. A Bristol express has passed Barnt Green and is heading for Blackwell with a typical double-header of 2-4-0 177 and 4-4-0 523. 177 has a Belpaire firebox, which was fitted in the late 1920s, but this did not prevent the loco being withdrawn in 1930. The summit of the Birmingham-Gloucester line was around here, at an altitude of 564 feet. The descent of the Lickey Hills lies a short way ahead. The bottom of the incline, at an altitude of 257 feet, was 3 miles 11 chains from the summit just mentioned. *Author's collection*

Ashchurch Level Crossing. 41061, a Bournville engine, approaches with a down local on 8 September 1949. The flat crossing going direct from Tewkesbury to Evesham is in the foreground – although no regular passenger trains used it in 1949, there was one daily timetabled working, the 7.25pm Evesham-Birmingham Central perishables, which came down from Evesham, across the flat crossing, then reversed through the Tewkesbury line platform, before gaining the main line and heading north. The reason for this manoeuvre appears to be because the train stopped at Defford for 13 minutes, presumably to pick up loads. Additionally the loco and stock of Redditch-Evesham-Ashchurch passengers used the triangle, of which the crossing formed part, to turn while there were excursions along it into the 1950s, one such being double-headed Compounds with a train bound for a women's hockey match at Wembley.

H C Casserley

Caprotti type 'Black Fives' which worked express passenger services. During 1957 the remaining ones were replaced by BR Standard class 5 4-6-0s, but Caprottis based at Leeds Holbeck and Derby still worked regularly on the line.

Brand new BR 9F 2-10-0s began to appear on freight workings from 1955 and from the summer of 1957 could sometimes be seen not just on summer Saturday extra passenger trains, but also on regular daily services. Eastern Region locos appeared from time to time – B1 4-6-0s Nos.61047 and 61113 were both seen passing through Cheltenham in June 1956 on special passenger trains – and this class reappeared with increasing frequency from the late 1950s, often three or four on a summer Saturday. In November 1959 V2 2-6-2 No.60954 caused great excitement by working through to Bristol on a scheduled express train from York, despite not being officially authorised to work on the line. The

following month, No.60839 also got to Bristol. Other LNER types appeared occasionally such as K3 2-6-0s, J39 0-6-0s, O1 and O4 2-8-0s, as well as at least two K1 2-6-0s, the first being No.62035, seen on 27 June 1963 on a down fitted freight at Cheltenham.

The last Compound on the route, 4-4-0 No.41123, was shedded at Gloucester Barnwood, often used as station pilot, but it managed to get out on express duties even towards the end of its life, being seen piloting the up 'Devonian' on 13 July 1959. It was withdrawn in December 1959. 2P 4-4-0s hung on a little longer, No.40489 being withdrawn from Barnwood in August 1960, while No.40540 still did pilot duties at Gloucester and was not officially withdrawn until early 1962, though latterly it was in store.

Pacifics in the form of BR 'Britannias' appeared fairly regularly, though 'Clan' 72005 was very unusual on the line in July 1960 with a summer relief working. There were appearances at least as far up as Gloucester by Southern Light Pacifics, with one making it through to New Street on the 'Pines Express' in December 1960. As dieselisation progressed on BR, some types formerly quite rare, such as 'Royal Scot' 4-6-0s, were transferred to depots like Sheffield Millhouses and Saltley, making them everyday sights.

While diesel multiple units had taken over many suburban services out of New Street in the mid-1950s, replacing various tank locos, main line diesels were not diagrammed for daily train workings until June 1961, in the form of Sulzer Type 4 1Co-Co1 'Peaks'. These were gradually introduced, starting with passenger and parcels, then express freight workings, though it needed Brush Type 4 Co-Cos to come along in the mid-1960s to secure guaranteed diesel haulage of such trains. Combined with cutbacks in main line and branch services and closure of goods yards, the writing was on the wall for steam.

The final date for 'normal' steam working on the line is not definitive – steam still worked some freight trains between Birmingham, Gloucester, Bristol and Bath or South Wales via Gloucester well into 1966, Sundays being particularly busy in the early part of the year, as backlogs of coal and other traffic were cleared. One railway society newsletter claimed that no less than 65 different steam locos were observed working at Gloucester in one week in January 1966, most, if not all, having worked down from Birmingham either via Ashchurch or Honeybourne – so much for the Western Region's stated aim of getting rid of steam on its lines at the end of 1965.... At least one regular express passenger was steam worked in 1966 following diesel failure, the 12.25pm York-Bristol on 19 January being seen at Cheltenham hauled by 'Black 5' No.45211 – this was a full four years after 'Modern Railways' magazine announced in its January 1962 issue that all class 'A' trains between Birmingham and Bristol would officially be Type 4 diesel-hauled! But steam on any trains at all, at least in the Cheltenham/Gloucester area, became less frequent as the year wore on and the last noted by the authors was on 14 September 1966 when an 8F, presumably working off Saltley depot, hauled a freight as far as Gloucester, going through Cheltenham around 7am, returning immediately light engine. (The very next day, preservation took a hand when No.7808 *Cookham Manor* – which had been a Gloucester Horton Road engine – left the Dowty Railway Preservation Society site at Ashchurch, under its own steam, to travel to Tyseley for a special working. However it did not go via Bromsgrove, but down to Cheltenham, then up the ex-GWR Honeybourne line). This was a month or so after the last regular steam working to Gloucester, a late night parcels train from Birmingham Snow Hill via the Honeybourne line, returning in the early hours, had gone diesel – it was usually a 'Black 5' in the last months of steam. There was a report that on 4 January 1967 Ivatt

2-6-0 No.46454 arrived at Gloucester from the north on a freight, again off the Honeybourne line, returning light engine. When Saltley shed closed to steam in early March 1967, the chances of any 'normal' steam working was virtually extinguished.

Train services

An 1853 timetable showed 17 daily trains from Gloucester to Birmingham: 10 goods; 4 passenger; 2 mail; 1 express. A typical stopping passenger service was the 7.0am from Gloucester which called at all stations, travelling along the 'Old Road' and the Camp Hill line to arrive at Birmingham Curzon Street at 9.58am. In 1934, the 7.0am from Gloucester travelled via Worcester Shrub Hill and the Birmingham West Suburban line, arriving in New Street at 9.28am. By 1960 it was departing Gloucester Eastgate at 6.52am, taking the same route as in 1934, to get into New Street at 9.27am.

In 1867, the fast services from Birmingham to Bristol, via Worcester, were doing the journey in 3 hours 5 minutes, while it took about 3 and a quarter hours in the other direction.

The line became very important as part of the cross-country railway network for long distance services from the North East and Midlands to the South West. In Queen Victoria's Diamond Jubilee year of 1897, the Midland introduced a new express from Bradford to Bristol utilising three sets of specially constructed, rather splendid carriages – four 12-wheeled and two 6-wheeled, all clerestory-roofed, in each set – with haulage allocated to a Johnson Single 4-2-2 locomotive, three being built for this particular service (one is now preserved, as No.673, by the National Railway Museum; this was withdrawn in 1928 from Saltley depot). Commencing on 2 August 1897, the southbound train left Bradford at 1.25pm; Leeds at 1.50pm; Sheffield at 2.53pm; Derby at 3.50pm; Birmingham at 4.55pm; Cheltenham at 6.0pm; Gloucester at 6.15pm, arriving in Bristol at 7.20pm. The northbound train departed Bristol at 2.5pm, arriving in Bradford at 7.50pm.

From July 1901 train services on the route were improved with more trains. A new weekday express left Derby at 8.54am; Birmingham at 10.15am; Bromsgrove at 10.41am; then via Worcester, Cheltenham and Gloucester, arriving at Temple Meads at 12.40pm. The best timing from Derby to Bristol was 3 hours 10 minutes, but a few years later, the 2.40pm from Derby arrived in Bristol at 5.37pm, a journey time of two hours 57 minutes, having stopped only at Birmingham and Cheltenham. Improved travel times owed something to competition from the GWR on its Birmingham – Bristol service, which amounted to four trains daily each way in 1914.

Through carriages were a big feature of the cross-country expresses. In 1905, the route saw, for example, through carriages from Liverpool, Manchester and Newcastle to Bristol; and Bradford and Leeds to

Southampton, Bournemouth and Torquay. The 2.20am Derby to Bristol had through carriages from Aberdeen, Glasgow and Edinburgh. The 12.40am mail train from Derby included postal vehicles through from Newcastle which were lettered 'M&NEJPS' meaning 'Midland & North Eastern Joint Postal Service'. A number of trains included restaurant and dining cars. In 1909 there were 14 long distance expresses north from Bristol to a variety of destinations, including Scarborough, Heysham for the Irish sailings, and Scotland. At Cheltenham, the Midland & South-Western Junction Railway provided an important link to and from Southampton with onward services providing connections to the 'Isle of Wight, Channel Islands, French Coast and Paris' as a contemporary advertisement proclaimed. Through carriages continued after the First World War, with workings such as Gloucester to Norwich, Yarmouth and Lowestoft.

1927 saw the title of 'The Devonian' bestowed on a long-standing train from Bradford and Leeds to Bristol. The train did not at that time run through to Torquay and Paignton the whole year round, but had through coaches when it did not, which were attached to a GWR train at Temple Meads. It departed New Street at 1.35pm, arriving in Bristol at 3.46pm, with stops at Cheltenham (on Saturdays) and Gloucester. The Winter 1934 timetable showed an altogether faster timing for this train – leaving New Street at 1.39pm, arriving at Temple Meads at 3.32pm – well under two hours – with daily stops at both Cheltenham and Gloucester. On summer Saturdays 'The Devonian' could run in four or five parts.

'The Pines Express' was the other named express familiar on the line for years. In 1927 the title was put on a train which had run from 1910 and went from Manchester and Liverpool to Bournemouth as a venture between the LNWR, MR and Somerset & Dorset. The service was suspended during the First World War, being revived in 1927. In 1934 it left New Street at 12.10pm, with stops at Cheltenham and Gloucester, before branching off at Mangotsfield for Bath, arriving at 2.15pm; from there it travelled over the Somerset and Dorset line. It used this route until September 1962 when it was diverted elsewhere.

In October 1937 trials for possible faster passenger train schedules were run from Bristol to Leeds and Glasgow and back using 'Jubilee' 5660 Rooke. On the northbound run on 12 October, the train of just over 300 tons took one hour 54 minutes between Bristol and Birmingham including station stops at Gloucester and Cheltenham and the usual stop at Bromsgrove for banking engines, one and a half minutes less than the test schedule. Overall running time of the test train from Bristol to Leeds, a distance of 205.9 miles, was 223 minutes, compared with a schedule of 229 minutes. This compared with the fastest timing by a service train over the route in 1937 of 245 miutes. Some fine running was also done on the return journey, but the strain on the Bristol Barrow Road engine

crew, particularly the fireman, was such that these times could not be perpetuated on a regular daily basis.

Birmingham-Bristol has also been a very busy freight route over the years. From the earliest days, when the railway provided an outlet via Gloucester Docks for Birmingham's industrial concerns, goods traffic to and from many parts of the UK found its way along the route. A few fast freights in latter steam days were: 2.55pm Bristol to York; 4.48pm Bristol St Philip's to Leeds Hunslet; 9.15pm Bath to Birmingham Lawley Street; 1.20am Tavistock to Crewe, via Worcester; 10.19pm Nottingham to Bristol St Philip's; 9.25pm Liverpool (Edge Hill) to Stoke Gifford; 4.20pm Burton Horninglow Bridge to Bristol West Depot.

Regional boundary changes in February 1958 saw most of the Birmingham-Bristol line come into the total control of BR's Western Region, only the section from Birmingham New Street to Barnt Green remained with the Midland Region.

Opposite, top: **Saltley, 26 April 1958**. With Saltley Sidings box in the background, locally based engine 48339 climbs quite vigorously albeit slowly past Saltley station on the Camp Hill line with a class 'J', loose coupled, freight. This could well have originated at Washwood Heath sidings less than a mile to the north and where so many freights to and from the Bristol route were sorted. Steam at the back of the train hints at a banking engine. Just a handful of goods trains conveying perishables – fish, fruit, vegetables, milk, chocolate etc. – traversed New Street station in normal circumstances, all other freight ran from Birmingham onto the Bristol route using the Camp Hill line to get to King's Norton.

Michael Mensing

Opposite, middle: **Saltley Junction, 9 April 1958**. A cross-country train which has come out of New Street and is headed for Derby and Sheffield passes the box at Saltley Junction behind Caprotti 'Black Five' 44745. 44745 had been a Bristol Barrow Road engine from July 1949 until May 1957 and saw plenty of use on the Bristol-Birmingham route. At 17A Derby shed when this picture was taken, it soon moved on again, to Liverpool. With the gasworks sidings on the left, the adjacent set of lines are for the Camp Hill route.

B W L Brooksbank / Initial Photographs

Opposite, bottom: **Duddeston Road**. 6985 Parwick Hall, from Gloucester Horton Road, 85B, heads off home, with Saltley Gasworks looming over the scene. The loco driver is looking back, probably checking that the freight's banker is in place, as the train prepares to attack the grade on the Camp Hill line. Following rationalisation of inter-regional freight workings in the early 1960s, ex GW type engines worked regularly from Washwood Heath on services such as the 12.25pm class H and 2.0pm class F to Stoke Gifford, near Bristol. *R Conway collection*

16

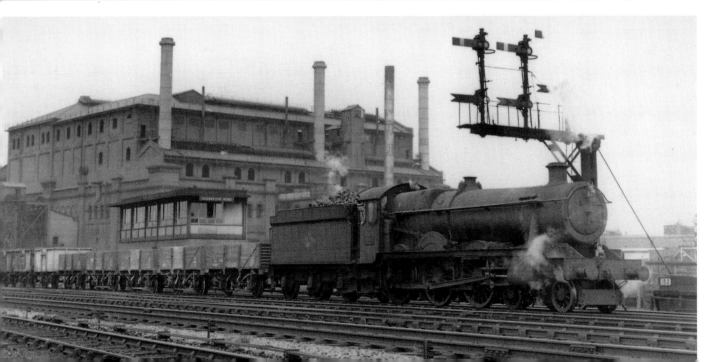

Saltley motive power depot. Engines from the large depot here always had lots of work on the Birmingham-Bristol line, so it is appropriate to pay a brief visit at the start of the journey. Midland and LMS 0-6-0s were the mainstay of the allocation and Saltley, 21A, 'Big Goods' 4Fs were seemingly ever-present at Bristol Barrow Road and Gloucester Barnwood depots or anywhere along the line. Passengers, parcels, fitted freights, loose-coupled coal trains – Saltley engines worked them all. When the Western Region tried to banish steam on its lines, Saltley engines, by now shed-coded 2E, would appear in Gloucester and Bristol to thwart those aspirations, before returning whence they came, sometimes in a string of five locos coupled together.

The allocation at 21A Saltley in January 1948		
0-6-0T 1F	4	
0-6-0T 3F	4	
2-6-2T 3P	4	
2-6-4T 4P	4	
0-6-0 2F	7	
0-6-0 3F	34	
0-6-0 4F	51	
0-8-0 7F	3	(exLNWR G2a type)
2-6-0 5F	19	
2-8-0 8F	16	
4-4-0 2P	6	
4-4-0 3P	2	
4-4-0 4P	4	
4-6-0 5P5F	19	
0-6-0D	4	
Total	**177 steam, 4 diesel**	

The scenes at Saltley are:

Right, above: The murky atmosphere of No.3 roundhouse viewed from above in September 1950 is fairly typical. The loco outside the shed on the right-hand edge, 0-4-4T 41879, was a Saltley engine at the time of this picture, but transferred to Bristol Barrow Road in March 1955, and was the last of its type there, being withdrawn in March 1960 after some time in store. The thrill of being in a big engine shed in the steam era is something that just cannot be recaptured by preserved railways – at least in the authors' opinion!
T G Wassell

Right, below: Johnson 2F 0-6-0 was 2994 in LMS days, becoming BR 58167.
T G Wassell

Below: Ancient Kirtley 2F 22853 lettered LMS survived into BR days and was allocated number 58112 but never carried it. Dating back to the 1860s, Kirtley 0-6-0s were a familiar sight on the Birmingham-Bristol route for years. 22853 still had double-frames, but had been rebuilt with a class 2 boiler.
F A Wycherley

18

Left and below: **Landor Street Junction and Brickyard Crossing, 25 October 1964.** The mass of lines around Landor Street would yield up some traffic bound for the B&G route which is to the right of the signal box. Behind the box are the lines from New Street to Derby with Lawley Street 'A' box in the background and Saltley beyond. Brickyard Crossing was south of Landor Street Junction and just north of St Andrew's Junction, where the line to Exchange sidings and New Street station curved off the Camp Hill line – and which was also used by B&G trains in the early days to Curzon Street station.
R J Essery collection / R S Carpenter

Right, above: **Brickyard Crossing, 19 June 1954.** Particularly on summer Saturdays, some passenger trains from the North and the East Midlands would escape the congestion around New Street by taking the B&G line through Camp Hill, joining the 'normal' route at Kings Norton. This applied to the up and down 'Pines Express' as well as reliefs such as the 8.8am Sheffield-Paignton seen here with 44848, while 44279 is heading the 9.30am Coventry-Wolverhampton towards New Street on the ex-LNW line. *T J Edgington*

Below: **Exchange Sidings, 23 December 1965**. These were put in for the exchange of goods traffic between the LNWR and MR, which commenced here in 1878. An ex-LNWR signal box controls movements at the sidings, situated between St. Andrew's Junction and Grand Junction (in earlier years Gloucester Junction, where the B&G linked up in 1841 with the Birmingham & Derby and the London & Birmingham to gain entry to Curzon Street station). Freights originating here in the early 1960s for the Gloucester line via Camp Hill included the 1.35am class 'E' and the 1.50pm class 'H' for Westerleigh. One incoming train was the 9.55pm class 'H' from Gloucester Barnwood, whose wagons might be marshalled onto services for destinations such as Coventry, Rugby, Kenilworth and various places in the Birmingham area – the Metro-Cammell works; Mitchell & Butler brewery; Oldbury; Curzon Street; Soho and so on.

N D Mundy

St. Andrews, 6 May 1956. 3F 43246 shoves hard at the rear of a southbound freight climbing through St. Andrews. The gradient hereabouts of 1 in 62, continuing at 1 in 85 to Camp Hill, meant that banking engines were available from Washwood Heath, some trains needed assisting as far as King's Heath. Going down could also be problematical – when 9F 92231 parted from its tender while on a descending train of 25 loaded Esso oil tankers on 14 November 1960, there must have been a few prayers said by the Gloucester Barnwood footplate crew – not to mention a few oaths!

Michael Mensing

Bordesley Junction, mid 1950s. This was the junction for the Great Western, whose line from Tyseley to Snow Hill went under the Midland's Camp Hill route in this vicinity. The GWR never had Garratt locos though! One can almost feel the earth shaking and the rails humming in this close-up of 47967 thundering past the signal box on its way to Kings Norton sidings. Garratts sometimes got beyond the West Midlands down to Westerleigh yard outside Bristol. One of the authors saw them on freight trains through Cheltenham in the 1950s on four separate occasions. *R S Carpenter collection*

Above: **Camp Hill station, 2 March 1936.** 0-4-4T 1348 of 21B Bournville depot calls with a set of suburban coaches on an afternoon service. The 2.0pm all stations from Kings Norton stopped here at 2.19pm, going non-stop to New Street, arriving at 2.26pm, while the 2.12 ex New Street, the train shown, left at 2.20pm, getting to King's Norton at 2.36pm. Some trains did not call at King's Norton, instead using the Lifford curve, on the circular service. *F A Wycherley*

Left: **Camp Hill station, July 1906.** This is the second Camp Hill station, replacing the original which became the Camp Hill goods depot. Everything looks neat and tidy in typical Edwardian era style. Note the two swan-neck water columns. Both pictures are facing Birmingham. With the separate goods warehouse, on the branch, there was no further need for this station when the passenger service was temporarily taken off in January 1941, never to be reinstated. *R S Carpenter collection*

Monday to Friday Camp Hill/Lifford circular service, 1934 *(not all station stops shown)* *Service also ran on Saturdays at slightly different times*				
New St	6.48am	7.54am		
Camp Hill	6.57am	8.2am		
Lifford	7.14am	8.13am		
Bournville	7.26am	8.21am		
New St	7.42am	8.34am		
New St	7.10am	7.52am	–	6.5pm
Bournville	7.26am	8.11am	5.21pm	6.17pm
Lifford	7.42am	8.20am	5.26pm	6.21pm
Camp Hill	7.58am	8.36am	5.41pm	6.36pm
New St	8.6am	8.44am	5.50pm	6.44pm

Timetable note: 'Season tickets between Birmingham New Street and intermediate stations to Lifford inclusive are available only by the Camp Hill route, and season tickets issued between Birmingham New Street and intermediate stations to Bournville inclusive can only be used by the Selly Oak route'.

Moseley station. Two views convey the charm of Moseley station in Midland Railway days. The first looks north as an 0-4-4T approaches on a local service from New Street. The second is looking south with the very unusually-shaped tunnel entrance prominent. The original Moseley station opened in November 1841, but became King's Heath station in November 1867 when this station came into use, just three-quarters of a mile further north!

Author's collection; F W Shuttleworth collection

Above: **King's Heath station**. The station looks delightfully rural in this view towards Camp Hill. The passenger service came off in 1941, but goods facilities were retained until May 1966. The signal box on the right opened on 30 April 1906 and lasted until 7 September 1969.

When he was at King Edward's Grammar School, Edgbaston, J R R Tolkien lived for a while in a house backing onto the railway at King's Heath and it is said that the names he saw on passing coal wagons – such as Nantyglo, Blaen-Rhondda, Penrhiwceiber – helped inspire the names and places he later used in his world-famous literary works 'The Hobbit' and 'The Lord of the Rings'. *Author's collection*

Below: **Hazelwell station**. This portrait is from 19 August 1929, looking towards Lifford. The station did not open until 1 January 1903. Closure to passengers took place in January 1941 and to goods on and from 1 March 1965. *Clarence Gilbert / R S Carpenter collection*

Inset: Detail from a Midland Railway System Map of 1913.

Above: **Lifford Station Junction, 1950s.** The junction signal box is on the left, with a 4F hauled freight heading towards Lifford from King's Norton, on the original Birmingham & Gloucester Railway line, while another 0-6-0 is on the Lifford curve, which links the Camp Hill line with the Bournville route into New Street. This useful, short, link enabled trains to arrive or depart at either end of New Street in the event of operating problems. It was also still used by goods trains from Washwood Heath to Central Goods, plus light engine movements and empty stock transfers.

Stations UK

Left: **Lifford stations.** The third station to serve Lifford, seen (top) on 1 July 1930 looking towards King's Norton, opened in September 1885 and like the first one, which lasted just a few years from December 1840, was situated on the Camp Hill line. The passenger service to and from New Street was halted during the Second World War, in January 1941, although the station closed to passengers a little earlier, on and from 30 September 1940. But it stayed open for goods until July 1964. The second Lifford station (below) was on the Birmingham West Suburban line and was also short-lived, only in business from 1876 to 1885 when it was bypassed by the new direct line from Bournville to King's Norton. This bypassed section became the Lifford Canal branch. The photo of the second station was taken in May 1958.

Clarence Gilbert, R S Carpenter collection; C H A Townley, J A Peden collection

Above: **Birmingham New Street, Queen's Hotel.** This was one way into New Street station – past the Queen's Hotel. The hotel, built by the LNWR and opened in June 1854, is shown here after enlargement between 1911 and 1917. Being right in the heart of the city, New Street, and the hotel, were always extremely busy.

Brunel University Transport collection, Clinker Views

Below: **Birmingham New Street, c.1910.** A scene inside the LNWR part of the station in the Edwardian era appears curiously devoid of passengers – perhaps they had been kept away while the picture was taken. From right to left the platforms are 1; 2/3; 4/5; 6. The Midland Railway on the other side of the station drive had platforms 7 to 11. The overall roof is very impressive, described as the largest single span example in the world when the station opened in 1854. But by 1945, with wear and tear, plus wartime bomb damage, it was decided to completely replace the roof on this side of the station, done in 1948. This view also shows the public footbridge which traversed the whole station.

Brunel University Transport collection, Clinker Views

Birmingham New Street. Another, somewhat less imposing, entrance was in Station Street, which gave access to the parcels office and Midland side of the station. The public footbridge is shown at the steps down to platform 7, again on the Midland side, with the BR style of direction signs prominent. *BR*

Above: **Birmingham New Street, 10 July 1925**. It is early LMS days, but this Kirtley double-framed 2-4-0 still carries its Midland Railway number 1. 2-4-0s were long familiar on the Birmingham-Bristol line. In 1930 number 1 was set aside for preservation and restored to its former Midland Railway identity as 156A, but was subsequently cut up. However classmate number 2, later LMS 20002, was restored as 158A and happily still survives today; it was exhibited at New Street during the station's centenary celebrations in June 1954.   *LCGB / Ken Nunn collection*

Below: **Birmingham New Street, 14 April 1949**. Horwich Mogul 2758 of Saltley depot, still sporting LMS on its tender, stands in the Midland side with the smartly-liveried B1 61325, which proudly displays 'BRITISH RAILWAYS'. Although of LNER design, 61325 was brand new to BR in June 1948, being allocated to Immingham shed. B1s became a daily sight from the late 1950s passing through New Street on the Birmingham-Bristol line, but in earlier times the only regular working for the class was a morning train from Cleethorpes to Birmingham.   *B W L Brooksbank / Initial Photgraphs*

Above: **Birmingham New Street, 1 October 1954.** 4-4-0s to the fore, with 21A Saltley's 40928 and 21B Bournville's 40463 awaiting duties. Until closure in 1960, Bournville shed provided engines for quite a number of the secondary passenger workings to Bristol. The photo has been taken from the west end of platform 7, with numbers 8 to 11 also in the view and the fish sidings on the far right. The latter were close to Birmingham Fish Market for which vans of fish arrived from Hull, Aberdeen and Fleetwood. There was a fish train on from here to Worcester and Gloucester, worked by a 2P 4-4-0 when seen on occasion at Cheltenham. Some Midland signals overlook the scene. *A G Ellis*

Below: **Birmingham New Street, 5 July 1958.** Platform 9 witnesses the arrival of the 12.52pm York-Bristol express with 'Jubilee' 45651 *Shovell* at about 4.0pm, while 4F 44553 stands alongside waiting its next duty, possibly the 4.35pm stopper to Gloucester Eastgate, judging from its class B headlamp. Both engines are allocated to 82E (formerly 22A) Bristol Barrow Road. The curve of the platforms shows up well. On the left is the elevated No.4 signal cabin. *Michael Mensing*

Above: **Birmingham New Street, 9 April 1959**. 17A Derby's Compound 4-4-0 41157 stands at platform 11 across from Bristol's 'Jubilee' 4-6-0 45662 *Kempenfelt*, which has charge of a down express at platform 10. The typical gloom of the station interior is evident beyond the 'Jubilee'. Although the reign of Midland Compounds on the route was drawing to a close, it is perhaps ironic that the last two of the type, 40936 and 41168, withdrawn in 1961, reposed at a former LNWR shed, Monument Lane, just beyond the New Street tunnels on the Wolverhampton line. This is a reminder that, as well as the Derby-Birmingham-Bristol route, the Compounds also worked Euston to New Street two-hour expresses for some years in LMS days. *R S Carpenter collection*

Below: **Birmingham New Street, c.1962/63**. 4-4-0s were but a memory when this shot was taken of BR class 3 2-6-0 76087 on a local from Worcester at the east end of platform 8 under the fine overall roof. A number of locos from this class were allocated to Saltley shed. Signal cabin No.2 can be seen behind the loco. In a few short years during the 1960s New Street station changed completely – not only was the building replaced by the new concrete structure – still gloomy – but steam also went, replaced by diesels, whose fumes pervaded the platforms no less than steam and smoke had done for a hundred years – as well as the electrics with their overhead wires and catenaries cluttering the view. That's progress! *A W V Mace collection*

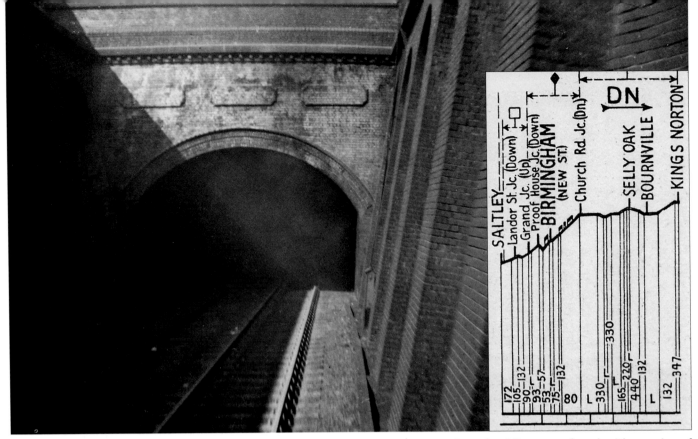

Above: **Five Ways, Bath Row tunnel c.1960**. Trains leaving New Street on the Bristol line were faced with a series of five tunnels in the mile or so to Five Ways, not to mention a climb of mainly 1 in 75/80. In steam days a banker was available to assist out of New Street. The tunnels always seemed to be wreathed in smoke and were damp as well, making progress difficult for any locos not in prime condition. Just one example – 45662 seen opposite, lost 35 minutes on 6 June 1960 while hauling the overnight Bradford-Bristol passenger mainly due to slipping in the tunnels because its sanders were not working properly. *D Ibbotson*

Below: The old Five Ways station closed in 1944, but a new one, seen here on 29 December 1983, was built on the site when the suburban service to Longbridge was revived in 1978. The diesel multiple unit is now history, replaced on the service by electric units. *N D Mundy*

Central Goods. At Five Ways was the branch to the Central Goods Station. Originally called Worcester Wharf Goods Depot, it was opened in July 1887, bounded on one side by Holliday Street and on the other by Suffolk Street. The name change came in 1892. The MR described it as 'the most central goods station in the city' and 'replete with every facility for promptly dealing with all descriptions of general goods and merchandise traffic.' After nearly 80 years serving Birmingham, the depot closed to traffic in March 1967.

The first picture is facing up the branch, with the lines from New Street at a lower level on the left. In the second portrait, Bournville's 43355 shunts vans in the Central goods yard. The third shows the goods depot on 26 September 1922, just in the pre-grouping era – and what a wonderful view! That was when railways really did the business. There are wagons from various companies all over the UK: NB, North British; LBSC, London Brighton & South Coast; GN, Great Northern; GC, Great Central; GW, Great Western; and of course MR. *D Ibbotson; R S Carpenter (2)*

Church Road. The top view, from 21 April 1929, is looking towards Five Ways, with the Central Goods branch on the right. From 1876 local passenger trains were able to use the Birmingham West Suburban Railway from Lifford to go to Granville Street station up the branch. Granville Street closed in 1885, when the connection from here to New Street was opened. The bottom picture shows Church Road station, which closed on and from 1 January 1925.

Clarence Gilbert / R S Carpenter collection; Institution of Civil Engineers

Above: Saltley had a stud of Ivatt Class 4 2-6-0s and one, 43063, powers a New Street to Redditch local at Pritchatts Road. This is not far from the old West Suburban station, Somerset Road. The Ivatts not only worked to Redditch and beyond to Ashchurch, but also to Bristol on stopping passengers and parcels trains, plus the occasional freight duty. They also appeared on reliefs like the Sunday evening 'as required' train which ran from New Street if the regular expresses were heavily delayed by weekend engineering works. *A W V Mace collection*

Below: **University**. Gloucester Barnwood's BR Standard 4-6-0 73092 sweeps round alongside the canal on a local from New Street to Worcester in 1963. This is the site for the University for Queen Elizabeth Hospital station, opened in 1978 and seen in the photograph overleaf, on 29 December 1983. *A W V Mace collection; N D Mundy*

Below: **University, 20 July 1963.** Not many through goods trains used New Street – it was crowded enough already with passenger services. The exceptions on the Midland side included workings from Austin's Longbridge plant and Cadbury's Bournville factory; one of the latter is featured here with 'Black 5' 44776 on an up van train just north of Selly Oak station approaching University Road overbridge. Perishables trains with fresh produce from Evesham heading for Saltley were also authorised on this route. The signal boxes at New Street were not allowed to accept a freight into their sections unless it had a clear road through, according to regulations. *A W V Mace collection*

Above: **Selly Oak**. This is the 1885 station, replacing the original of 1876 and the view south is from the up, Birmingham, platform. The signal box beyond the station on the down side appears to be of modern design, making it the one opened in January 1958, replacing an earlier box. It was taken out of use in August 1973.   *Stations UK*

Below: An up passenger, 1E38 to Sheffield, has B1 61394 of 41D Canklow shed as motive power, as it approaches the station in the early 1960s; note the slightly staggered platforms here.   *A W V Mace collection*

Above: **Bournville, 16 April 1955**. A 'Trains Illustrated' excursion passes through heading for New Street behind 44842. This had 'Castle' class haulage up the Lickey bank, but, as the advert noted – 'the class is prohibited from Birmingham New Street' – hence a change of power was made outside Bournville mpd. On the right is the connection to Bournville motive power depot, 21B. Behind the train is Bournville signal box, while the left-hand line is the Lifford canal branch. This branch was used for trains to Granville Street from King's Norton – commencing in April 1876 and lasting until the direct King's Norton-Bournville line opened. It was then downgraded to a siding.   *R S Carpenter collection*

Left, above: **Bournville, 4 March 1961**. Passing the chocolate factory, travellers might have caught a glimpse of a well-kept locomotive or two shunting. Cadbury's was a big railway user for many years and had a fleet of engines, both steam and diesel. The three seen here are Cadbury's No.10, No.1 and No.6. The saddle tank was not much more than five years old at the date of this photo. Built in 1955 at Pecketts of Bristol, it came here by rail, passing through Cheltenham on 31 August 1955 hauled by 2-6-2T 8106. The two side tanks were also from Bristol, built by the Avonside Engine Co in 1925 and 1923 respectively. On 16 February 1963, No.1 was towed down the Bristol line as far as Ashchurch, where it was preserved at the Dowty site, situated in the sidings adjacent to the old Midland Railway provender store. It is now at Tyseley, Birmingham. Rail traffic at the factory ceased in May 1976.   *J Peden*

Left, below: **Bournville station**. The view, across the Worcester & Birmingham canal, shows some work being done on the down platform with what looks like a new shelter extension. An engineers train is working wrong line. The chocolate factory is behind the trees on the left. An overbridge from the factory crossing the LMS line and the canal was constructed a little north of here enabling Cadbury's to shunt its trains to a warehouse alongside the canal. At one time public and trade excursions by train to Bournville from various parts of the country were very popular – one such was on 23 August 1961, through Cheltenham with 'Jubilee' 45663. The station, suitably updated for today's commuters, remains open.   *Author's collection*

Bournville motive power depot.

Above: A view inside the roundhouse in May 1958 reveals engines of four different classes, all allocated to Bournville. From the left: Compound 40925; 4F 44203; Stanier 5MT 44981; 3F 43523, pretty representative of motive power here at the time. For most of the 1950s there was one 8F, 48523, which had a regular freight working to Gloucester. Another Bournville engine familiar down the line was Fairburn class 4 2-6-4T 42186 with a morning stopping passenger. For some time, a small jet of water sprayed out of a hole in its left-hand side tank! The shed, which opened in March 1894, closed in February 1960 and the site was taken over by Cadbury's. *RAS Marketing*

Left, above: On 2 March 1935, Kirtley double-framed 0-6-0 2603, fitted with a class 2 boiler, poses alongside the coal stage. Four of the class, though not 2603, survived into BR days – one at Saltley shed and the other three here. The late survival of the type was due to their use on the Halesowen branch, which included a particularly spindly viaduct, restricting the line to locos with a light axle load. *H C Casserley*

Left, below: An ex-London Tilbury & Southend Railway 4-4-2T is here on 17 July 1935, complete with 21B shedplate. Ten of the type had recently been transferred to the Birmingham area after being displaced by new Stanier 3-cylinder 2-6-4T on their home ground. In turn, they helped replace Deeley 0-6-4T, which had been associated with the Birmingham area but were all withdrawn by 1938. *Midland Railway Trust*

The allocation at 21B Bournville in January 1948	
2-6-2T 3P	5
2-6-4T 4P	4
0-6-0 2F	6
0-6-0 3F	7
0-6-0 4F	4
4-4-0 2P	2
4-4-0 4P	4
Total	**32**

Above: **Bournville, 16 April 1955**. Bristol Barrow Road's 'Jubilee' 45651 *Shovell* hurries the 12.15pm York-Bristol express towards the Breedon Road overbridge. This stretch of line, from Stirchley Street & Bournville (as Bournville station was then called) to King's Norton was opened on 26 September 1885, giving a more direct route between the two than the canal line via Lifford. *T J Edgington*

Below: **Lifford West Junction, 16 April 1955**. This is the empty coaching stock of the 'Trains Illustrated' tour seen earlier at Bournville. While the excursionists had an hour's break at Birmingham, the ecs was sent on a gentle amble via Camp Hill to come back into New Street near departure time rather than clog up a platform there. This short section linking the Camp Hill and Bournville lines was known as the Lifford curve, opening on 1 July 1892 when the circular New Street-Bournville-Camp Hill-New Street and vice-versa passenger service was introduced – in 1903 there were nine such trains on weekdays, basically for morning and evening peak traffic. It was also used for light engine and empty stock movements, plus freights and trip workings making their way through Camp Hill to Bournville, Selly Oak and Central Goods. *T J Edgington*

Above: **King's Norton, Midland Railway days**. The staff pose for a portrait on the up platform, while the station displays lots of interesting paraphernalia in this view looking towards Lifford. The down platform had rather more imposing buildings, constructed when the station was enlarged to cater for trains on the Birmingham West Suburban Railway; this was probably also the time that the raised sections at the far end of each platform were built. The signal box by the overbridge (more visible in the next photograph) is presumably elevated for sighting purposes.

Author's collection

Below: **King's Norton, Midland Railway days**. Heading through the station is 2-4-0 126 of shed 3, Saltley, with empty stock, possibly bound for the carriage sidings here. The photo was taken prior to the widening work which took place in the mid-1920s, two new lines being put in on the left, enabling the separation of traffic to and from the Birmingham West Suburban line and the Camp Hill route.

Author's collection

Above: **King's Norton, early 1960s.** A two-car Metro-Cammell dmu is on a stopping train for New Street at platform one, while a group of trainspotters are gathered on platform two. During the 1950s diesel multiple units took over a lot of the steam suburban passenger workings out of New Street, which had used 2-6-2T and 2-6-4T. This view shows well the effect of the widening done in 1924-26, with the new station and two lines on the left coming into use on 14 March 1926. The main flow of passenger trains was via Selly Oak, but some through passenger trains used the Camp Hill line to avoid New Street, particularly in the summer, while the regular 5.15pm stopper from Bristol took this route into New Street for some years, as did a Saturdays only evening passenger from Ashchurch via Redditch.

The second picture shows one of the two booking offices adjacent to platform one, built as part of the 1920s scheme.

Joe Moss collection / R S Carpenter

Above: **King's Norton, early 1960s.** An intruder in the shape of Great Western 4-6-0 4972 *Saint Brides Hall* heads an express freight bound for Washwood Heath via Camp Hill. 4972 is traversing the lines seen on the right in the photograph opposite. 'Halls' were permitted to work over running lines between Abbot's Wood and Water Orton or Lawley Street via Camp Hill, or via Selly Oak, subject to various restrictions. They were also permitted into New Street, but only on certain platform lines and sidings. Ex-GWR types were fairly common here in late steam days, even working local passenger trains from Gloucester and Worcester into New Street, while one of the GW 0-6-0PT bankers regularly worked a local freight up from Bromsgrove to Washwood Heath. On the left of the picture can be seen carriage sidings, the main ones for the Midland side of New Street.   *Joe Moss collection / R S Carpenter*

Below: **King's Norton.** A local train pounds away from King's Norton towards Northfield behind Deeley 0-6-4T 2031 and a rake of suburban carriages, probably a Redditch service. The loco was in a class of 40 introduced in 1907 and many were based in the Birmingham area for local workings. They proved to be unsteady at speed, one derailed in 1935 at Ashton-under-Hill while working a service to Ashchurch, which, following similar incidents with the class, hastened their demise and all were withdrawn between 1935 and 1938.   *Author's collection*

Northfield, c.1912. The station in the top view is the 1893 one, with a single island platform, which replaced the original two-platform station of 1870. The two outside lines, up and down goods, were installed between King's Norton and here in 1892, being extended to Halesowen Junction in 1894, and were worked on the permissive as against the absolute block system of the passenger lines. This meant that passenger trains would not normally be allowed to use them. The modern view is dated 6 August 1983 and depicts the expanded station which came into use in May 1978, with platforms now serving all lines. *Author's collection / N D Mundy*

Above: **Halesowen Junction**. An up express has just passed the junction with 3P 4-4-0 714 at the head. Part of the Austin car factory is in the background. The coaching stock is of a mixed profile, appropriate for a train no doubt having through carriages from and to a variety of places. For a number of years, 3Ps were the mainstay of the heavier expresses on the Birmingham-Bristol route. 80 of the class were built from 1900 to 1905, with most, including 714, being rebuilt by Fowler with superheaters from 1913. The 4P Compounds did not appear on the line until the mid 1920s, after the LMS recommenced building them following the Grouping. *W L Good / Author's collection*

Below: **Halesowen Junction, 29 May 1935**. 0-6-0 3817 crosses from the down goods line, with the signal indicating it is heading for the Austin Motor works at Longbridge and the Halesowen branch. The way that the train is marshalled suggests that the first few wagons and brake van might be the branch goods, while the rest of the train is for the car works. The Halesowen branch was vested jointly in the MR and GWR. Ordinary passenger trains from King's Norton over the branch to Halesowen ceased as early as 1919, though excursions, and workmen's trains to Austin's, ran for many years afterwards. Ordinary freight traffic to Halesowen survived until 1964; the branch connection remains in use today solely for Rover car traffic. *H C Casserley*

Above: **Longbridge, 6 August 1983.** With an increasing population in this part of Birmingham, it is perhaps surprising a station at Longbridge on the main line was not opened until 1978; that was on the site of the original short-lived Longbridge station which existed in the 1840s. The suburban service has now been electrified through here and out to Redditch.

N D Mundy

Below: **Longbridge, 20 March 1924.** This joint MR and GWR station was on the Halesowen branch, opening in 1915, at a time when the Austin works was expanding rapidly to produce war material. The view here is looking towards Halesowen Junction. Sidings for goods trains off the branch into the works were in place by August 1915 and over the years, vast numbers of cars and materials needed for their production, have travelled by rail. The rail sidings became a large complex and Austin Motors / British Leyland owned steam shunting locos for many years, until 1973. The works is still rail connected and has its own fleet of diesels.

Author's collection

Above: **Longbridge, 25 June 1952**. The joint nature of the station shows in this photograph, with a Great Western 0-6-0PT, No.7428, awaiting a rush of Austin workers on the service to Old Hill, on the GW beyond Halesowen, while a train of LMS carriages in the other platform is bound for Saltley. Hanging around at the station is not encouraged by the rather rudimentary shelters! The workman's service to Old Hill was withdrawn on and from 1 September 1958; the one to Saltley lasted a little longer, ceasing on and from 4 January 1960. In 1949, there was a morning arrival from Saltley and an evening return, while there were two morning trains from Old Hill and two evening returns, with several empty stock working, as well. There was also a parcels train arrival in the morning from Birmingham Central and an evening return.
C H A Townley / J A Peden collection

Below: **Longbridge, June 1931**. Johnson 1P 2-4-0 No.262 approaches Halesowen Junction with an up stopping passenger train. It is passing a disused platform which was opened in 1918 during the war for use by factory workers. There was also a platform on the down side. Both closed in 1922, though the up side's was extant for many years. Although rebuilt with a Belpaire firebox a few years earlier, 262 had been withdrawn from service by 1934.
Author's collection

Cofton Hackett widening, late 1920s. The Midland wanted to put in extra running lines from Halesowen Junction to Barnt Green and demolish the narrow Cofton Hackett tunnel, a scheme which came to fruition in LMS days. Two pictures illustrate the works in progress. A 3F and 4F are employed for works trains, while a contractor's 0-6-0ST is at a higher level. The contractors were Messrs. Logan and Hemingway, who had two Manning, Wardles at the site and their loco shed is in the second picture, upper right. Cofton Hackett tunnel was demolished between 10.15pm on 26th and 6.45am on 28th January 1929, according to historian C R Clinker, and replaced by this cutting. But it was May 1930 before the two new lines to Barnt Green came into use. The Austin Motor factory at Longbridge is in the background.

J A Peden collection / R S Carpenter collection

Above: **Barnt Green, 1950s**. Saltley's 'Crab' 42823 trundles away from the station with a Gloucester-New Street service. The line to Redditch, Alcester, Evesham and Ashchurch veers off left, the distance to Ashchurch being 32 and three-quarter miles. The direct main line route from Barnt Green to Ashchurch was 27 and a half miles, though the service offered between the two places meant going via Worcester, adding another two and a half miles to the journey. As for time taken, the 4.59pm from Barnt Green, on the Gloucester stopper via Worcester, got travellers to Ashchurch at 6.13pm; or they could go on the 5.37pm via Redditch and arrive at Ashchurch at 7.8pm.

R S Carpenter collection

Below: **Barnt Green, 11 May 1963**. Ivatt 2-6-0 43122 has just left the main line with the 1.12pm Saturdays only New Street to Redditch; this service had been mostly diesel multiple units since April 1960. Passenger trains no longer ran from Redditch to Alcester, while from there to Evesham had closed completely – due to the poor condition of the track, a substitute bus service operated from 1 October 1962. The section from Evesham to Ashchurch stayed open, usually worked by an engine and one coach, but the passenger service was withdrawn on and from 17 June 1963, with full closure of the section being in September 1963, apart from a short stub into the military depot at Ashchurch.

R M Casserley

Above: **Barnt Green, 12 July 1939**. 2-6-2T 16 waits with the 7.43pm Redditch-Birmingham train. These engines were introduced by Fowler in 1930 and during the decade replaced the Deeley 0-6-4Ts, four of which were shedded at Redditch in 1934. The 'Stephens Ink' and 'Virol' adverts were familiar at railway stations for years, while the LMS advertisement on the building extols the virtues of visiting places on the Evesham line on Sundays. Excursions to Evesham from Birmingham used to be very popular. On Whit Monday 1962, there were eight specials advertised – some steam-worked, some dmu. Another went beyond Evesham to Ashchurch with steam, but the return was shown as a dmu in BR's working notices.

H C Casserley

Below: **Barnt Green, c.1910**. A delightful Midland Railway scene, out in the country setting of Barnt Green, which had only a handful of inhabitants when the station first opened in 1844. The double-header is on the down main line. Note the staggered platforms, the up one was moved in 1927 to the position shown in the 1950s photograph. The Redditch line curves away on the right. A group of people are just leaving by horse-drawn carriages in the left background. Note the very tall signal post on the up side. The leading engine is 680, one of Johnson's magnificent single-wheelers, in pristine condition.

Stations UK

Blackwell, c.1920. 2P 4-4-0 517, of shed 8, Bristol, heads a southbound express in Midland Railway days. Until November 1941 there was a compulsory stop for down passenger trains prior to descending the incline. Then the requirement became one of reducing speed to 10mph. A couple of 0-6-0T bankers, including 1947, are waiting to return to Bromsgrove. Bankers never coupled to the train they were assisting – or to each other – and would just drop off after the train had breasted the summit. They would then wait for a suitable path back down the incline. 1947's later life included working through Metropolitan Railway tunnels in London, for which it was fitted with condensing apparatus.

R S Carpenter collection

Above: **Blackwell, 12 July 1939**. An LMS built 4-4-0, 630 of 22B Gloucester depot, waits in the loop for the signal to start gingerly descending the Lickey incline, when the resident brakesman and train guard will pin down brakes on a previously agreed number of wagons, by the use of brakesticks. The loco's tender brake would also be applied. Going down with a loose-coupled freight like this one was more fraught than ascending the incline and a 4-4-0 would perhaps not be a driver's first choice for such a job. Possibly the outward working for the loco was a passenger duty. The passing freight has a Southern Railway wagon in its consist.

H C Casserley

Below: **Lickey Incline, 6 June 1925**. 4-2-2 672 of shed 3, Saltley, assists an up express headed by 4-4-0 543. The locos and carriages are fairly typical of the early LMS period. The varied coaching stock in this and the next picture is noticeable – as well as carriages of MR origin, there would be examples every day of GWR, LNWR and other pre-grouping railways' stock on through services. The next few years would bring big changes – the regular appearance first of Compounds, then of Stanier locos and carriages.

Author's collection

Lickey Incline. *The* banker was 'Big Bertha', built at Derby specially for the job in 1919. This unique 0-10-0 spent virtually its whole life shoving trains up the bank, with occasional forays to Derby for overhaul or to Gloucester for attention on the wheel drop, though it did have a short stint on Toton-Brent coal trains in 1924. Here are two shots of it in action, one as LMS 2290 and the other as BR 58100. In 1947 it was renumbered 22290, becoming BR 58100 in January 1949. It was withdrawn in 1956, leaving Bromsgrove on 7 May for Derby, a sad day indeed. Drivers on 58100 had to be careful when buffering up to a passenger train, so as not to hit it too hard. In October 1952, for example, a Bromsgrove driver received a severe reprimand for 'causing sharp contact with rear of 2.12pm Bristol-York when banking, complaints received from passengers.' *Ken Nunn collection, LCGB; R K Blencowe collection*

Above: **Lickey Incline, 31 August 1955.** Leeds Holbeck 'Jubilee' 45573 *Newfoundland* thunders up the Lickey on the Cardiff-Newcastle express with assistance from no less than four 0-6-0Ts blasting away at the rear of the train. The four are 47303, 47502, 47313 and 47305. While three of the tanks are Bromsgrove's own, 47313 is a Saltley engine, perhaps borrowed during a busy period or covering for a loco under repair. The coaching stock is a mixture of LMS and GWR, 12 vehicles in all; this train regularly loaded to 370 tons or more, often being double-headed from Gloucester, where the LMR took over from the Western Region. *R K Blencowe collection*

Right, above: **Lickey Incline.** The new big banker after 58100's demise was a BR 9F, 92079, which inherited the former's headlamp. Various other 9Fs also did banking duties over the remaining years of steam and in this picture it is 92230 pushing a freight up the incline. A few other types also appeared as banking engines in the late steam era, the most long-lived was ex-GWR 2-8-0T 5226 which arrived in May 1958, remaining until April 1960. Some short freights were allowed to ascend without a banker – 8 loaded mineral wagons; 12 loaded goods wagons; or 16 empties. *R K Blencowe collection*

Right, below: **Lickey Incline, 13 June 1964.** A stopping passenger service from Bristol to Birmingham, 2M74, has 'Black Five' 44965 at the front, with assistance from 0-6-0PT 8402 at the rear. By this date, with diesels taking over more and more workings, 44965's train was actually diagrammed for diesel haulage. This relatively light load, just five coaches, would surely not have taxed 44965 unduly if it had made a solo ascent of the bank, but regulations required a banking engine if the train was more than four bogie vehicles. Trials were held in March 1955 with a 'Jubilee', 'Black 5' and a BR Standard class 5MT on unassisted trains of over 200 tons up the bank, but nothing came of these tests. *R K Blencowe collection*

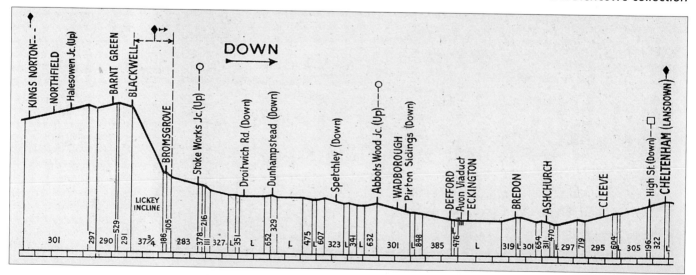

Above: **Lickey Incline, 12 July 1939**. Compound 1058, of 22A Bristol depot, coasts down towards Bromsgrove station with a lightweight express, signalled into the platform road. In late 1938, 1058 was in a collision with 'Jubilee' 5565 at Derby for which a Bristol passed fireman received a severe reprimand. *H C Casserley*

Below: **Bromsgrove station, 12 July 1939**. 'Three Freight' 0-6-0 3506 of 22B Gloucester eases its goods train through the platform road, with the crew looking pretty relaxed. It was not always so – bringing a loose-coupled freight down the Lickey could be a hair-raising experience if the engine lost control of the train. Many's the time that stopping precisely at the water column at Bromsgrove South was thwarted by the speed of the train overcoming the engine's brake, with a resulting overshoot of the column. Then after stopping it was often not possible to reverse the train, so the loco would uncouple and run light along an adjacent road back to the water column, thus wasting time, with the crew being asked to explain why at the end of their shift. A couple of known examples of this – Bristol Driver Davies got a caution on his record dated 4 June 1931 for 'Overrunning water crane, Bromsgrove South' with engine 3183; one of his colleagues, Driver Huntley, received a caution on 4 September 1931 for the same offence with engine 3181. *H C Casserley*

Bromsgrove.

Bromsgrove was pretty much a railway town from 1840 onwards, with a large number of people employed in various capacities. It was chosen by the Birmingham & Gloucester Railway as the site for its locomotive works. After takeover by the Midland Railway, Bromsgrove works was turned over to wagon construction and maintenance. It underwent a big expansion in the 1870s, employing around 600 men and became one of the Midland's main wagons works outside of Derby, the work done there being held in high regard through the years.

In 1880 Bromsgrove had 11 engines for banking duties, including four 0-6-0WTs built at Derby in 1860-63 specially for the work. In 1905, 16 passenger trains each way called at the station on weekdays, compared with 1872 when 10 northbound and 8 southbound stopped there. While Johnson 0-6-0 tanks provided the mainstay of the banking engines for many years, the need for a larger locomotive to cope with increasingly heavy trains

resulted in Derby Works building a special 0-10-0 tender engine which arrived at Bromsgrove on 20 January 1920. An LMS Beyer-Garratt put in a brief appearance on banking trials in early 1934. The Johnson tanks lasted as bankers into the 1940s, eventually being transferred away and replaced by LMS built 'Jinty' 3F 0-6-0T. The 0-10-0, 'Big Bertha', numbered 58100 in BR days, remained as Bromsgrove's big banking engine until being withdrawn in May 1956. It saw off visits from the LNER's sole Garratt No.69999 which was not a success as a banking loco here. When 'Big Bertha' went, its replacement was BR 9F No.92079 and a few others of the same class were also used until steam bankers officially finished, replaced by diesels, and Bromsgrove shed closed in September 1964. The other big change in later steam days was the replacement of the LMS 0-6-0Ts by GWR type 0-6-0 pannier tanks, most notably Nos. 8400 to 8406 inclusive. Over the years various classes of loco had usually short-lived trials as bankers or were pressed into service in times of shortage.

Bromsgrove shed and works, August 1922. The Midland Railway loved 0-6-0 tender engines; at 31 December 1922 it had 1598 of them, including 471 Kirtley double-framed examples. The immaculate 2905 illustrated here was an early Johnson one, a 2F of the '1142' class; it was built by Kitson in 1875 and numbered 1147 prior to 1907. 2905 appears to be pretty much in original condition with round-topped firebox, Salter safety valves, square panel over the rear driving wheel and small Johnson cab. From 1875 until 1908, no less than 935 0-6-0s were built for the Midland – over the years there were variations, some were 2F, some the larger 3F, some built or rebuilt by Deeley and so on. And from 1911 Fowler introduced his class 4 0-6-0s of which there were 192 on the Midland at the Grouping, many more being constructed during the LMS era.
R S Carpenter collection

Right, above: **Bromsgrove shed and works, 6 January 1957**. The loco depot shows various changes from the 1922 view. Gone are the curved brick arch openings and the fine wall lamp, while a shock awaits in the locos themselves – GWR type pannier tanks have recently arrived to take over from the 'Jinty' 0-6-0T. A whole batch of 0-6-0PTs from 8400 to 8406 inclusive arrived between November 1956 and January 1957, and the faithful 'Jinties' started to drift away to other depots from December 1956, though they were still represented at Bromsgrove in reduced numbers for some years. During 1958, the depot's shed code changed from the Midland Region's 21C to the Western Region's 85F, reflecting the latter's extension of its boundary on the Bristol-Birmingham route as far north as Barnt Green.

H C Casserley

Right, below: **Bromsgrove, 1949/50**. Even 'Big Bertha' looked small compared with ex-LNER Garratt 69999, which arrived in March 1949 to work on the Lickey. The massive 2-8-8-2 had been built in 1925 for banking duties on the Worsborough incline in Yorkshire, but electrification did it out of a job there. It was not popular at Bromsgrove, among other things needing a lot of coal shovelled to do the job, so it went away in November 1950. It was converted to oil firing in 1952 and returned to Bromsgrove in July 1955 for another unsuccessful spell of about two months, after which it went away again and was withdrawn in late 1955. In this portrait, 69999's home shed, painted on the buffer plank, is still shown as Mexboro.

R S Carpenter collection

Below: **Bromsgrove, 1950s**. Another unusual resident at the shed, allocated from November 1952 until withdrawal in March 1955, was ex-Caledonian Railway 0-4-0ST 56020. Its purpose was to heat oil for use with the Garratt, but as 69999 was not there, 56020 was really redundant before it started! In this picture 56020 has a rag cover over the chimney denoting its stored status. It was replaced by ex Lancashire & Yorkshire 0-4-0ST 51217, which presumably did the work in the short period that the oil-fired 69999 was in use at Bromsgrove.

Joe Moss collection / R S Carpenter collection

Left, above: **Bromsgrove, 18 July 1964.** Another loco type which would have caused great excitement ten years or so earlier was the ex-LNER 'B1' 4-6-0, but these became common on the route from the late 1950s. Canklow shed's 61370 restarts a heavily loaded summer Saturday relief towards the Lickey incline with assistance from the banking locos. The train was 1N79, 7.50am Paignton-Newcastle, typical of the many extras run for holidaymakers. 61370 had worked down the previous evening on 1V49, 7.30pm Sheffield-Newquay. 1964 was the last summer with a goodly number of steam-worked class A passenger trains; by the following year, steam was much rarer, even on these summer reliefs. *A W V Mace collection*

Left, below: **Bromsgrove, 12 July 1939.** Here is a busy scene at the same location as the previous picture, from the other side of the tracks. The signal layout is the same, though the arms and gantries are of earlier types. The three 0-6-0Ts on the main line are 7443, 7235 and 7425. There is a goods train on the down, while a 'Big Goods' 4F awaits the call to ascend the incline, with another banking loco alongside it. *H C Casserley*

Below: **Bromsgrove South, 1954/55.** A 'Jinty' stands ready to do battle with the Lickey, while 58100 waits patiently for work at the coal stage, located on the up side. For trains not booked to stop at Bromsgrove station, banking engines assisted from here after February 1914. There are some nifty bits of pointwork in the foreground, enabling various movements on and off the main line and sidings. In later years an oil terminal was built on the up side towards the station, providing regular trains for some years into the diesel era. The large factory on the left was the engineering firm of Garringtons, which was rail connected at the time. *Joe Moss collection / R S Carpenter collection*

The allocation at 21C Bromsgrove in January 1948	
0-6-0T 3F	8
0-6-0 2F	2
0-10-0	1
Total	**11**

The allocation at 85F Bromsgrove in March 1959	
0-6-0PT	7
0-6-0T 3F	2
0-6-0 3F	1
2-10-0	1
Total	**11**

Stoke Works. Along with Droitwich, Stoke Works was, and still is, famous for salt, produced at the Salt Union works, situated adjacent to the down main line. This superb view of the junction and works was taken before the main line widening in 1932/33. The sidings are full of vans and wagons for the salt traffic, including a few with the distinctive pitched roofs. The signal box seen here was closed on 5 March 1933 after the widening work, replaced by one situated a little further north of the junction. The GWR had running powers across the main line to gain access to sidings at the works. In BR steam days, there was still a Monday to Friday train conveying salt on a trip working to Droitwich and Worcester, worked by a GW loco.

F W Shuttleworth collection

Above: **Droitwich Road.** This station on the 'Old Road', originally called Droitwich, opened on 24 June 1840; the name change occurred from 10 February 1852, but the station closed to passengers on and from 1 October 1855. A February 1852 timetable shows six trains each way stopping on weekdays, with three on Sundays. It remained open for goods until 1 October 1952. This undated view is looking north. The milepost on the up platform indicates 60 and a quarter miles from Derby. *R&CHS*

Below: **Droitwich Road, 3 May 1963.** In the 1840s the GWR had the desire to advance the broad gauge north by taking over the Birmingham & Gloucester Railway, but the B&G instead became part of then-new Midland Railway company. For many years GWR type locos were uncommon on the original B&G route through Dunhampstead and even in the mid-1950s it was a matter of note if one was seen ascending the Lickey incline. But gradually they infiltrated, with pannier tanks stationed at Bromsgrove for banking and the Western Region of BR taking over the line to Barnt Green. This photo shows 6800 *Arlington Grange* on a short semi-fitted freight approaching Droitwich Road and heading towards the Lickey and Birmingham. It returned next day through Cheltenham on a down freight working. *Michael Mensing*

Spetchley, 10 March 1950. This was another early station opening on the 'Old Road', on 24 June 1840, and early closing – to passengers on and from 1 October 1855. In those heady early years, it was the station for Worcester, reached by an uncomfortable three-and-a-half mile ride by stage coach. But once the Oxford, Worcester & Wolverhampton line from Abbot's Wood opened on 5 October 1850, the MR was able to run directly into Worcester. Gough's *Midland Chronology* records that excursion traffic for Spetchley Park continued to use the station after closure. Goods traffic lasted until the start of 1961. Between Droitwich Road and here, there were other early stations: Dunhampstead – where just one train each way stopped except on Sundays when there were two; Oddingley and Bredicot. *R&CHS*

Above: **Stoke Works, 17 April 1959.** Stoke Works station was situated on the Great Western line from Droitwich and was unusual in that GWR passenger trains never used it. The Midland had, since OWW days, running powers over the 'Worcester Loop' from Stoke Works Junction through to Abbot's Wood Junction via Droitwich and Worcester Shrub Hill. In very early days there was a station on the main line here, but along with several others on the 'Old Road' to Abbot's Wood, it was closed to passengers after a few years. This view is looking towards the nearby 'Old Road' at Stoke Works Junction, and Bromsgrove.   *R M Casserley*

Below: **Stoke Works, 17 April 1957.** Some gangers stand aside as the 7.35am Nottingham-Bristol via Worcester passes with Saltley's 45269 and Derby's 'Patriot' 45509 *The Derbyshire Yeomanry*, which was the regular engine for this train. It might be doing 45509 an injustice to speculate that the 'Black Five' was attached to assist, but the 'Patriot' had a bit of a reputation as a poor steamer during its time as a Derby engine. The train going north on the other track is the 9.24am Great Malvern-New Street. For some years 45509 was the only regular 'Patriot' on the Birmingham-Bristol line. It was transferred away in the summer of 1958, but at the end of that year, three of the class – 45504, 45506 and 45519 – came to Bristol Barrow Road shed.

Droitwich Spa, c.1910. A beautiful portrait of the Midland Railway in its pomp – Elgar's *Land of Hope and Glory* exemplified. Johnson 1P 2-4-0 174, a Saltley engine, departs from the station with a Great Malvern to New Street express – perhaps the great composer was a passenger on occasion, travelling from his Malvern residence. This MR service was introduced on 1 July 1896 running via Worcester Foregate Street and Stoke Works; as a wartime economy, it was withdrawn on and from 1 January 1917. It took until 8 June 1953 for the service, glimpsed at Stoke Works in a previous picture, to be restarted!

R S Carpenter collection

Above: **Droitwich Spa, c.1920**. A nice array of advertisements adorn the neat station here with its red brick buildings constructed in the 1890s and replacing the original wooden station. Droitwich was on the Oxford, Worcester & Wolverhampton, as well as being the junction for the approximately four mile line to the Midland's 'Old Road' at Stoke Works. An 1867 timetable noted that local passengers between Worcester, Fernhill Heath and Droitwich were not carried by Midland Railway trains. A GWR loco is in the station in this view looking north.   *Stations UK*

Below: **Fernhill Heath, c.1920**. Situated between Droitwich Spa and Worcester was this tranquil station. So tranquil that no New Street-Worcester-Gloucester-Bristol trains at all called here, at least in latter steam years. For instance, the slowest up passenger in 1960 was the 6.52am Gloucester via Worcester to New Street, arriving there at 9.27am, but even that service missed out Fernhill Heath. However a 1934 LMS timetable shows that particular train did stop here and it was marginally faster from Gloucester to New Street – by seven minutes! A few other LMS services also called in 1934, though not as many as halted at Droitwich.   *Stations UK*

Above: **Worcester, 1950s**. 22A Bristol 4F 44536 makes sure of leaving its mark on Worcester as it departs past the loco shed with an up local for Bromsgrove and Birmingham under a huge cloud of black smoke. In October 1959, 44536, a long-time Bristol engine, was transferred to 5D Stoke-on-Trent.   *P Chancellor collection*

Below: **Worcester, 4 June 1965**. 'Black 5' 45264 stands on the 'five whistle road' (down goods avoiding line) with a class E company train from Margam to Rood End, which it would take up through Droitwich and Stourbridge Junction, not Stoke Works and the Lickey. Diesels were in the ascendancy by this date on most types of trains, but this one was still shown in the working time table commencing 14 June 1965 as steam hauled – and the scene in this picture is still pretty steamy. In the right background is the ex-GWR loco shed, while on the left is part of the former Oxford, Worcester & Wolverhampton Railway's loco, carriage and wagon works.

Above: **Worcester Shrub Hill, 1971**. The fine frontage of the station has been obscured by various less pleasing structures, as well the inevitable car park. Shrub Hill had been a joint station between the GWR and Midland Railway and there was also about a mile of jointly-owned track through the station, from a point adjacent to the MR's loco depot to just beyond Tunnel Junction, where the GW line from Hereford and Worcester Foregate Street came in. Both railways had their own goods stations here. The Midland Railway used to run quite a lot of freight trains via Worcester onto the Hereford line, but in LMS days, they were diverted to the North and West route through Shrewsbury. Consequently the LMS closed its loco shed here in 1932. *Stations UK*

Below: **Worcester Shrub Hill, 14 April 1959**. 'Crab' 42839 arrives from the north with a parcels train. Worcester loco shed, 85A, is behind the train, with an assembly of ex-GW types – though LMS engines also used it from 1932 when that railway's depot here closed. The 'Crab' has just passed the junction from Worcester Foregate Street station and the Hereford line, coming in from the left. *B W L Brooksbank, Initial Photographs*

Above: **Worcester Shrub Hill, 7 July 1964**. Motive power for the 7.4pm Gloucester – New Street local is 'Jubilee' 45579 *Punjab*. This was due away from Shrub Hill at 8.26pm and would travel via Bromsgrove. In the background is Shrub Hill Station signal box, while in the platform nearest the camera, up – to London – in GW parlance but down – from Derby – for the Midland, a DMU operates another service. 45579 had been an old faithful on the Birmingham -Bristol line, but was withdrawn the month after this photograph was taken. It made at least one more appearance though – on 21 July it was in charge of an empty stock working, 3X33.   *P Chancellor collection*

Below: **Worcester Shrub Hill, 1890s**. Immaculately polished 2-4-0 126 stands with a down Midland express. This engine, renumbered 126A in March 1899 and 121 in 1907, was one of the famous Kirtley '890' class, rebuilt by Samuel Johnson. 126 had been Birmingham-based since 1880 and apparently was still there when withdrawn in 1924, so was likely to have been a regular visitor to Worcester.   *R Fraser collection*

Above: **Worcester, 27 May 1937**. The little-photographed LMS engine shed stands empty, having been closed on and from 12 December 1932. It was opened by the Midland Railway in 1870 and had a fair-sized allocation, but became a victim of changed traffic patterns and economies in the difficult circumstances of the early 1930s, which resulted in the Pooling of Traffic Agreements between the big railways in 1932. At least some of the shed staff found employment elsewhere on the LMS – one Alfred Tummey who had been a coalman at Worcester depot since 1907 transferred to Bristol Barrow Road shed on 12 December 1932 as a shed labourer, before becoming a coalman there in 1934.

W A Camwell

Below: **Worcester, 15 June 1960**. A double-header – shades of Midland Railway practice, though of course it used smaller engines – consisting of 45265 and 45654 *Hood*, moves the 10.45am Sheffield-Bristol away from Shrub Hill past the Metal Box Company factory. Metal Box has been an important railway customer for many years, as witnessed by the vans in its siding.

Above: **Norton Halt, 16 February 1963**. Saltley's 45186 hauls the Esso tank train empties, which have come from Bromford Bridge, north of Washwood Heath, and are going to the refinery at Fawley near Eastleigh. When these working started in 1960, they were routed via the 'Old Road', Gloucester South, Bristol and Westbury, but now travelled as previously to Stoke Works, then through Worcester and Oxford before taking the Didcot, Newbury and Southampton route to get to Fawley. Eastleigh shed, 71A, had a batch of 9F 2-10-0s for the workings, though engines from Saltley depot – whether its own or 'borrowed' from another shed – predominated whichever route was used and often worked through to the Southern Region! *P Chancellor collection*

Below: **Norton Halt**. This was on the Worcester Loop, just off the 'Old Road' at Abbot's Wood, which, in this view, is on the line to the right. The line to the left is the Worcester-Oxford route. The Midland Railway called this Norton Junction Station, but in latter steam days at least, no Bristol-Birmingham trains called here.

David Lawrence, Hugh Davies collection

Above: **Abbot's Wood, 24 July 1950.** Barrow Road's Midland Compound 41028 is homeward bound with a stopping passenger working, just south of Abbot's Wood Junction, whose signal box can be seen in the distance. Just visible behind it is the Worcester-Oxford line which goes from left to right. In the early days of the Worcester Loop, there was a short-lived exchange station at Abbot's Wood Junction, originally called Worcester Junction.

B W L Brooksbank, Initial Photographs

Below: **Wadborough.** Just 1 mile 20 chains from Abbot's Wood Junction was Wadborough station, well looked after by the staff, one of whom is peering out of a doorway. The station closed on and from 4 January 1965. The two-storey building is a relic of the Birmingham & Gloucester Railway – note its closeness to the line. It still exists today.

David Lawrence, Hugh Davies collection

Above: **Defford, 21 June 1962.** Saltley's 44137 passes with a down minerals – at 4.55pm according to a note on the photograph. This indicates that the up train, performing a shunting move to collect traffic, is 5M22, Gloucester Barnwood to Lawley Street, sometimes diesel-hauled by this date. Just over a year later, on 1 July 1963, goods facilities were withdrawn from Defford and other stations in the area. *Author's collection*

Below: **Defford.** Three and a half miles south of Wadborough was Defford (for Pershore). The view is looking north. Goods traffic is to the fore in this portrait from Midland Railway days, which contains a wealth of interest – the people, the structures, the rolling stock – displaying a way of everyday life now gone. This is a picture literally worth a thousand words, which repays close study and thinking of past glory. Pride was still evident in the 1950s, as railway writer G. Freeman Allen commented 'Defford station was worth a second glance, for the staff have done their best to make a pleasant garden of the down platform; the usual railway benches have been replaced with garden seats that are neatly framed in rock-walled flowerbeds; and the whole display has been given a neat touch with a sundial.' *B Matthews collection*

Above: **Eckington, early 1950s.** The railway crosses the River Avon before arriving here, just over a mile away from Defford. This view north is probably half a century later than the one at Defford, but still neat and clean. The box on the down platform opened in 1892, downgraded to a ground frame for the crossing in 1969, before going out of use in December 1972. *Joe Moss collection, R S Carpenter collection*

Below: **Eckington, 7 August 1956.** Evening light shines on a Gloucester-New Street stopper as it arrives behind 21B Bournville depot's well-kept 40917. Sadly 40917 was withdrawn in December 1956, an indication of changes which would sweep away the old order of motive power on the route in a few short years. *P J Shoesmith*

Above: **Bredon, 15 October 1960**. The 8.15am Newcastle-Cardiff hauled by two 'Jubilees', 45683 *Hogue* and 45639 *Raleigh*, with steam to spare and a clear signal would have been more than capable of sustained running at the maximum line speed of 75 miles per hour. This train was allowed 31 minutes for the just over 31 miles from passing Bromsgrove to stopping at Cheltenham, pretty much the average for expresses at the time. It was often double-headed; for a three-day period in the late 1950s, it was memorably hauled by Compound 41100 and 'Patriot' 45500.

B W L Brooksbank

Below: **Bredon, early 1950s**. The four wayside stations from Wadborough to here, a total distance of just under seven and a half miles, all served a prosperous area of agriculture and market gardens, and had their own varying characteristics, as is obvious from the pictures. This view of Bredon is looking north. Loads of boxes for local produce are dumped on the down platform.

Joe Moss collection, Roger Carpenter

Ashchurch. With steam to spare, 3P 734 starts away across the famous level crossing on a northbound local passenger train. Withdrawn in October 1949, it never carried its allocated BR number, 40734. Ashchurch Level Crossing box, behind the engine, opened in October 1927, not only replacing an earlier box which was on the up side north of the crossing, but also those at Tewkesbury Junction and Evesham Junction, which were at the west and east ends of the level crossing. The crossing itself was opened as double track in October 1864 and singled by 1927, being finally taken out of use and removed in 1957.
P Chancellor collection

Above: The fine Midland Railway water tower, with workshops underneath, happily survives to this day alongside the new Ashchurch station, opened in the 1990s. *D Ibbotson*

Below: **Ashchurch, late 1940s.** 'Three Freight' 0-6-0 3507 displays a good head of steam as it blasts north on a heavy mixed freight. The Midland Railway canopy is prominent on the down platform, while on the up side the sturdy construction of the station buildings is evident, all in all a fine example of Midland architecture. The sign on the up platform lists the stations with connections from Ashchurch – 'Tewkesbury, Malvern, Evesham, Alcester, Redditch'. But the '& Stratford-on-Avon' has been painted out, as the passenger service to there from Broom Junction, on the Evesham-Alcester-Redditch line, ceased 'temporarily' from 16 June 1947 (the cessation was made permanent from 23 May 1949), although the section remained open for freight. *Author's collection*

Above: **Ashchurch, 29 May 1950**. GW engines regularly worked through, as witness Mogul 5348 passing with an excursion from its home, Hereford, to Dudley via Gloucester. This class of engine was specifically prohibited from running between Barnt Green and New Street, so the train would be going via Worcester and Kidderminster. The up side building is prominent again. There was a refreshment room which also served as the local pub, much frequented no doubt by troops coming and going at the adjacent large military depot, just along the Evesham branch, during the Second World War and for some time after the conflict ended. *B W L Brooksbank*

Below: **Ashchurch, 26 July 1947**. Compound 1039 of Bournville depot is captured turning an Evesham line train. Having arrived at the Evesham line platform on the opposite side of the station, 1039 would have taken its train, of 3 or 4 coaches, onto the main line, then reversed, as seen here, onto the Tewkesbury line, propelling back past the platform to Tewkesbury Junction. Then it would draw forward over the flat crossing to regain the Evesham line, before shunting back into the Evesham line platform, all ready to depart. *B W L Brooksbank*

Above: **Ashchurch, 1 November 1951**. It was still possible to travel from Ashchurch through to Great Malvern via Upton-on-Severn when 0-4-4T 58071 was photographed leaving on its one coach, 'one class only' train. The service was cut back to Upton-on-Severn from 1 December 1952; only local protests stopped the passenger service on the whole of the branch being chopped at that time. 58071 is just joining the flat crossing at Tewkesbury Junction. The building on the left is the former Midland Railway provender store, which provided feed for the company's many horses in earlier days. 58071 is still fitted with a condensing pipe, which betrays an earlier life working London commuter trains through Metropolitan Railway tunnels. It also retained Salter safety valves until withdrawal from Gloucester Barnwood depot in 1956. *B W L Brooksbank*

Below: **Tewkesbury goods yard, early 1920s**. We are trying not to stray too far from the main Birmingham route in this book, but could not resist including this picture at Tewkesbury. It depicts Kirtley double framed 0-4-4 well tank 1206, which looked ancient even in the 1920s, the class to which it belonged having been built in 1869/70. Our excuse is that passengers at the time could well have seen this loco at Ashchurch performing Malvern branch duties, which it did for many years. 1206 was withdrawn in 1927. In very early days Tewkesbury branch trains were hauled by horses and later was notable for using the last working Norris 4-2-0 on Birmingham-Gloucester territory, of course well before the branch was extended through to Malvern in May 1864. *R S Carpenter collection*

86

Above: **Ashchurch, looking north**. This is the classic view from the main road overbridge. The Tewkesbury and Malvern line goes off left, with the Evesham line curving away right and the main line to Birmingham going straight ahead on the racing stretch which, with easy gradients, enabled non-stop expresses to roar through at high speed, an impressive sight for people on the platforms. There was a goodly railway community here, with over 100 people in the Midland Railway's employ in 1910. Apart from station and train staff, there used to be four signal boxes, plus the provender store, track gang and assorted other duties to provide employment. Some workers lived in back-to-back railway houses here, while the stationmaster was provided with a large residence just north of the station.

B Matthews collection

Right: **Ashchurch, early 1950s**. Some fine Midland signals grace the landscape south of the main road and the station. The nearest track is the up main. There were (and still are) some sidings here on the down side, for which up trains had to propel back over the crossover seen in the picture. This was a dubious manoeuvre given the speed and frequency of main line trains and led to the tragic accident on Tuesday 8 January 1929 in which four people died and 25 were injured. The up 7.20am express from Bristol to Leeds with Compound 1060 overran signals in thick fog and collided with a goods train setting back from the up to the down line. Such was the extent of the wreckage that the line did not reopen for traffic until the Thursday morning.

R S Carpenter collection

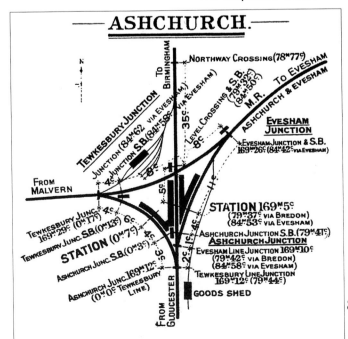

87

Above: **Cleeve, c.1949**. Again looking north, this wayside station, as can be seen, was a modest affair. Approximately halfway between Ashchurch and Cheltenham, it closed on and from 20 February 1950. The house on the right still exists to mark the site for modern-day passengers.

W Dendy

Below: **Cheltenham High Street, 20 February 1963**. The severe winter of 1962/63 caused British Railways great problems, not least in the motive power situation. Diesels had been steadily advancing their share of trains worked from Birmingham to Bristol, but steam substitution was often required due to diesel non-availability in the frequently freezing conditions. Approaching High Street signal box is the diesel rostered 1V38, 10.28am Sheffield-Bristol, hauled by 45625 *Sarawak* whose home shed is 24L Carnforth, so well away from its normal haunts. Indeed this period was very good for seeing rare engines on the route, as normal diagrams were disrupted not just by failures but also late-running trains, which meant that locos, and crews, could not keep to their assigned duties. Consequently any available engine was grabbed for a train which needed a loco.

R Stanton

Above: **Cheltenham High Street, 20 February 1963**. Saltley engines were of course seen en masse, so 43940 is more typical as it steams along on a down coal train. Between the siding on the right and the road bridge was the site of Cheltenham High Street station, which opened on 1 October 1862 and closed on and from 1 July 1910. Also here were the MR's goods yard, the Midland & South Western Junction Railway's loco shed and the sidings of Cheltenham Gas Company, so it was a busy area. *R Stanton*

Below: **Cheltenham High Street, c.1949**. The High Street goods yard pilot poses for a picture taken by Walter Dendy, who was goods agent here at the time. 47607 had an interesting past, having been shipped to France in March 1940 for war duty as WD number 10. But it came under German control after the Dunkerque retreat. Remarkably it survived the war and returned to the UK along with four other 'Jinties' in August and September 1948 in a bad state of repair, entering Derby Works for renovation, including getting rid of bullet holes! 47607 was allocated to 22B Gloucester Barnwood from 20 November 1948. *W Dendy*

Above: **Cheltenham High Street, c.1949.** Walter Dendy was on hand to take this photograph of ex-Somerset & Dorset 2-8-0 53800 outside the old Midland Railway goods shed. Still displaying 'LMS' on the tender, 53800 could well be heading north to Derby Works for overhaul. Perhaps one of the last of the type to pass through Cheltenham in BR steam days was ex-works 53808 on 14 August 1962. While 53800 did not last into preservation – though thankfully 53808 has – the goods shed is a remarkable survivor in the year 2001 and is now a listed building. *W Dendy*

Below: **Cheltenham, Alston Junction.** This Midland box, north of Lansdown station, dates from 1891, and is another survivor, having been turned into a ground frame in 1968, also controlling a busy road crossing. There was a coal wharf here and access to sidings which were used jointly by the MR and MSWJR.   *R K Blencowe collection*

Above: **Cheltenham, Alston Wharf, c.1949**. The sidings are still in use for passenger trains starting and terminating at Lansdown. Trains for the ex-MSWJ line to Andover and Southampton stabled here until November 1958, when the service transferred to Cheltenham St. James' station. For some reason, these sidings were known as 'The Creek'. The goods in the background of this picture is on the down loop and it was not unusual in steam days for the loco fireman to leap off as his train trundled to a halt, run over the main line, climb the fence and disappear into the nearby Midland Hotel to obtain liquid refreshments for himself and the driver! 41903, probably Lansdown station pilot, did not linger long in the area, being allocated to Gloucester Barnwood between 15 October 1949 and 22 July 1950, when it went to Derby. In the later 1950s, many enthusiasts flocked to Ashchurch to see sister loco 41900, the last of the class in service, which worked the Upton branch for a period.   *W Dendy*

Below: **Cheltenham, 12 May 1961**. Ex-Crosti 9F 92026 heads the Esso tank train empties on its journey from Bromford Bridge, Birmingham, to the Fawley refinery, near Eastleigh. Another Esso train flow through Cheltenham was from Avonmouth to Bromford Bridge. This view, looking down on 'The Creek', is taken from the approach road to the former Cheltenham & District Tramways depot, which was used for buses by the time of this picture. *R Stanton*

Above: **Cheltenham Spa Lansdown station, mid 1960s**. Many have been the complaints since its opening in 1840 that Lansdown station is not really good enough for a town as distinctive as Cheltenham – in the wrong place, too far from the town centre, drab and dingy internally, and so on. But it is a listed building and if BR ever had ambitions to replace it, these fell foul of the planners. It has undoubtedly always been a very busy station with a relatively high proportion of prosperous travellers buying first-class tickets. The nine-bay Doric colonnade which graced the frontage was removed in 1961. The entrance does look shabby in this portrait; every few years the station receives a coat of paint and remedial work, but remains basically unaltered up to the present day. *RAS Marketing*

Below: **Cheltenham station, early 1900s**. A delightful Johnson single-wheeler poses at the north end of the station. 32 was constructed at Derby in 1888, a member of the 25 class, with 7'4" diameter driving wheels. Single-wheelers were regular performers on the route for years, being used mainly as pilot engines on expresses after the First World War and 43 of them survived into LMS days, the last being withdrawn in 1928. *Author's collection*

Above: **Cheltenham Spa Lansdown station**. The title of the station until February 1925 was plain 'Cheltenham'. This view is at the Gloucester end looking north, with the up platform on the left. Today's station would basically be recognisable to a traveller who knew it in the nineteenth century. One bugbear for years was that express trains had to draw up due to the short length of the platforms. These were eventually extended at this end in 1964/65 to overcome that problem, doing away with the sidings in the process. Probably the other biggest alteration in recent years has been the construction on both sides, just behind this view, of somewhat out-of-scale buildings for the Royal Mail's parcels operation.   *B Matthews collection*

Below: **Cheltenham Spa Lansdown station, 24 June 1956**. Bristol Barrow Road 'Jubilee' 45690 *Leander* is in charge of a down express. Barrow Road had a fleet of well-maintained 'Jubilees' for working a number of the principal expresses on the Birmingham-Bristol line, including through workings for both engine and crew to and from Leeds. The old signal box on the right at the entrance to the down bay platforms was latterly used as a storeroom. The bay came into use in January 1900, but it is not known to the authors when it ceased to be used for passenger trains. During the Second World War, the LMS stabled two coaches in the bay to assist the YMCA in providing sleeping accommodation for servicemen passing through the town.   *E R Morten*

Above: **Cheltenham Spa Lansdown station, 1949.** Ex-Midland 2-4-0s had been reduced to just three examples, built by Johnson, when BR came into existence in January 1948 and it was a surprise when one, LMS 20216, the l. with 6'9" driving wheels, was transferred to Gloucester. It spent time at Lansdown as station pilot, becoming a bit a celebrity, and was even photographed by the local newspaper. There was a need for a vacuum fitted engine station pilot, capable of shunting vehicles on and off passenger trains, which may be why 20216 was selected for t job – perhaps nothing else was available at the time. 20216 was allocated a BR number, 58022, but was withdraw in 1949 without carrying it. Here the veteran sits in the bay sidings from which some MSWJ trains used to depa Behind the wall can just be seen a signal, which is on the ex-GWR Honeybourne line. *W Den*

Below: **Cheltenham station.** An express train rolls towards the up platform with a 4-4-0 loco which is not from t Midland Railway, but from the Midland & South Western Junction Railway. It is one of nine built by the North Briti Locomotive Co and delivered between July 1905 and June 1914. Most were based at Cheltenham MSWJ loco shed working trains to and from Southampton. Some MSWJ services included through carriages for destinations such Liverpool and Manchester, which would require shunting here, by the tank loco in the siding, onto an MR tra Adverts proclaimed the MSWJR/MR as forming 'the shortest, quickest and most direct route between Paris, via Hav French Coast, Channel Islands, Southampton, Portsmouth and the Midlands, North of England and Scotland.' *A B MacLeod/NF*

Incidents and Accidents

Things did not always run smoothly in the good old days of steam. Crews would have some explaining to do at the end of their shift after these incidents and accidents along the line...

6 March 1901, Washwood Heath. Driver Clutterbuck and Fireman Richards were both reprimanded for failing to observe that a signalman had lowered the wrong signal, moving off and damaging a point.

26 February 1918, Saltley loco sidings. Driver Holloway was reprimanded for causing a collision between engines 92 and 475. (Engine 92 was a Kirtley (rebuilt Johnson) single-framed 2-4-0 class 1P; 475 was a 2P 4-4-0)

26 November 1908, Brickyard Crossing. Passed Fireman Welsford was suspended for 6 days after his train passed the home signal at danger and collided with the rear of a goods train.

11 August 1905, New Street. Driver W Parsons was suspended for 4 days after passing a starting signal at danger.

26 November 1921, New Street. An express from Bristol to the north, due New Street at 4.27pm, crashed into the rear of a stationary Tamworth and Derby train. The Midland 4-4-0 on the express hit the local's back coach, a 6-wheeler, which was cannoned into the next coach, a bogie vehicle, whose body was broken with part being pushed up to lodge against the footbridge.

26 October 1910, Church Road Junction. Driver Penney was reprimanded after his engine derailed at the end of a short siding.

23 December 1935, Selly Oak. Driver E Hill was cautioned for leaving the train's guard behind after carrying out rule 55 – train engine was 4-4-0 Compound 1000.

30 May 1896, King's Norton. Fireman Cantle got a caution and Fireman Richards had to attend an enquiry after their excursion train was turned onto the goods road (due to the signalling system in use on the up and down goods lines here, passenger trains were not permitted to run on them, so the engine crew should have stopped and questioned the routing for which they were erroneously signalled.)

5 June 1928, Cofton tunnel. Driver W Jones was reprimanded for not complying with speed restrictions. (This was during the time that work was underway to remove the tunnel.)

16 September 1957, Barnt Green. A Barrow Road fireman was reprimanded for not maintaining steam and water on his engine working the 4.45pm Bradford-Bristol mails, causing delay.

22 October 1908, Lickey Incline. Driver Bright and Passed Fireman Rogers were cautioned after bad judgement in drawing over the brow at Blackwell caused their train to overrun Bromsgrove.

28 December 1909, Bromsgrove. Driver Bright was fined 2/6d for not stopping at Bromsgrove and over-carrying passengers.

9 February 1920, Stoke Works. Driver King was suspended for 1 day – due to mismanagement the boiler of his engine, 92, became short of water, a lead plug fused and the firebox was damaged.

19 August 1929, Droitwich. Driver Usher was cautioned after overshooting the platform on the Derby passenger, with 2P 4-4-0 522.

9 September 1952, Dunhampstead. Driver Sperring had a caution after passing the up home signal at danger, while working the 2.15pm Bristol-York express.

13 September 1927, Spetchley. Passed Fireman Swift got a caution after a fire iron he was using on 0-6-0 3F 3169 came into contact with another engine.

25 July 1902, Worcester. Fireman Cooper was suspended for 6 days for not being in a fit state to work his train and being under the influence of drink.

May 1950, Defford. A disaster was only just averted when the 4.48pm Worcester to Gloucester passenger train was struck by an RAF Meteor jet which was landing at the adjacent airfield. The locomotive's cab was dented by the jet's landing wheels! The driver and fireman, and some passengers, suffered from shock, but were able to proceed with the train.

25 November 1937, Eckington. Driver Ludwell was suspended for 2 days for overrunning signals.

6 August 1960, Bredon. A Gloucester Barnwood driver and fireman received a 'Disciplinary Form 1' after 4F 43924 dropped a plug while on the 5.45pm Birmingham-Bristol stopping passenger.

30 July 1928, Ashchurch. Driver Beake was cautioned for not carrying out rules and not discovering his train, with 0-6-0 3F 3444, had divided.

21 May 1906, Cleeve. Driver Lewington was fined 1/- for disregarding instructions re engines whistling. (There were various whistle codes to be given when passing here for relaying to signal boxes further on, e.g. if a passenger train was not stopping at Cheltenham, 2 long, 1 crow; if a freight train was stopping at Cheltenham for traffic, 4 long; if a train was going via Gloucester South Junction, 1 long, 2 short; etc.)

27 August 1908, Cheltenham. Driver Maggs had a caution for not testing the brakes before leaving.

*Details have been taken mainly from personnel records and loco casualty reports. **Dates in bold** are the actual dates of the incidents shown. Other dates are those entered on the personnel records – the incidents could have occurred anytime from same date to several weeks previously. Most of the crews mentioned were based at Bristol Barrow Road shed. No doubt men from other loco depots which worked the line over the years had similar misadventures!*

Selected Bibliography

Birmingham & Gloucester Railway *Rev. W Awdry*
(very detailed history of the early years)

Railways of the West Midlands – A Chronology
C R Clinker

The Story of New Street *F W Grocott*

The Railway History of Bromsgrove and the Lickey Incline *Bromsgrove Steam Enthusiasts Club*

The Lickey Incline *H C Casserley*

Birmingham & Gloucester Loop *J M Tolson*
(in November and December 1964 Railway Magazine)

Passengers No More *G Daniels & L Dench*

The Midland Railway – A Chronology *J Gough*

Midland Railway System Maps

Track Layout Diagrams Section 34 – Birmingham to Cheltenham *R A Cooke*

Trains Illustrated
November 1951; January 1955;
January, February, March 1957.

Midland Record

Midland Railway and LMS Time Tables

BR Working Time Tables and weekly notices

Acknowledgements

The authors thank everyone who has helped in the preparation of this work, but in particular: Mike Randall who, with many years firing and driving on the route, has been able to assist with various matters; and Midland Railway Society member Peter Witts who has also generously offered advice about things Midland from his extensive knowledge. Further information about anything contained in this book is always welcome.

While every effort has been made to obtain permission from owners of copyright materials reproduced herein, the publisher would like to apologise for any omissions and will be pleased to incorporate missing acknowledgements in any future editions.

Worcester Shrub Hill, 5 August 1932. An historic view showing the overall roof, which was removed in the mid 1930s.
V R Webster, Kidderminster Railway Museum